Mind The Gap!

Analyze and Improve Performance

WILLIAM E. BEANE, Ph.D.

FOREWORD

Execution is the great unaddressed issue in the business world today. Its absence is the single biggest obstacle to success and the cause of most of the disappointments that are mistakenly attributed to other causes.

LARRY BOSSIDY AND RAM CHARAN
"Execution: The Discipline of Getting Things Done"

WHY THIS BOOK?

I have spent the last 20 years optimizing the performance of managers and employees. During the 1990s, my efforts were focused on sales managers in a large international Bank. They constantly complained about their salespeople. In the process of working with them, I made three observations.

First observation: The sales managers were quick to assign blame, yet seldom understood why salespeople were struggling to reach their numbers. They also failed to understand their own role in the struggles.

Second observation: Attempts to diagnose the causes of poor performance typically focused on a deficiency on the part of the salesperson. Among the most common diagnoses were: "...He doesn't care...she's not trying hard enough...he's got a bad attitude." In other words, they were saying that the salesperson was "broken" and therefore had to be "fixed."

Another common diagnosis was: "They need more training...he needs a class on this...she should go to a workshop on that, everyone needs more training..." This kind of thinking morphed the problem into a training issue. So the sales managers held training accountable for maintaining performance rather than themselves.

Third observation: The managers were largely oblivious to their role in either enabling or disabling the performance of their salespeople. Very seldom would they ever question what they, themselves, were, or were not, doing that could have contributed to the problem. They were eager to take partial credit for good performance, but didn't see themselves implicated in poor performance.

This problem of finger-pointing is incredibly pervasive. The pattern of blaming the performer without noticing one's own culpability, in fact, seems to be a core component of much managerial DNA.

Managers surmising that a salesperson was "broken" and needed to be "fixed" typically approached attempts to coach with all the delicacy of a jackhammer. The most common approach was to fixate on the diagnosis (for example, doesn't care, has attitudes, is lazy, seems demotivated), then make fixing the diagnosed problem the key focus of the coaching.

In fact, the sales managers often were attempting to fix the wrong problem—in other words, coaching the wrong issue. As a result of such failed coaching, managers tended to generate more push-back than progress.

Take a look at most performance books. They're relatively complex, theoretical and written primarily for consumption by "other performance theorists." Few managers are eager to dive into a heavy textbook on "performance analysis and improvement." You'll discover it's difficult to find anything systematic, much less easy to learn and apply—anything that has the bandwidth to handle a wide variety of challenging human performance issues.

Look no further. The following pages fill that void.

This book, in addition to outlining an analysis and improvement system, also serves as a performance management job description for any manager, at any level, detailing how to *Mind The Gap*: Define any gaps in performance between the actual and ideal, identify who or what is causing the gap, and take the actions necessary to close the gap.

The factors of the Performance-7™ system outline what effective managers should do, on a continuous basis, to ensure peak performance across their teams. Minding the gap makes less effective managers more effective and raises the bar for effective managers, taking them to even higher levels of performance.

Employees and managers who work for a company that takes performance leadership seriously and practices the P-7 principles can expect to see a work environment far ahead of the curve

Attention would be paid to tasks, assignments and processes. Everyone would have a clear, realistic, agreed-upon picture of expectations and priorities.

People would receive regular, constructive, balanced feedback to ensure accountability, keep performance on track and provide recognition to build pride in a job well done. Adequate training and development would ensure that everyone had the skills and knowledge necessary to handle assignments successfully.

Motivated employees would perceive gains from a job well done and could take pride in accomplishing tasks importance to the organization and its customers. People would be assigned to jobs they were capable of handling—ones that best utilized their individual talents and strengths. If personal issues became a problem, troubled employees would receive HR assistance to help them cope more effectively.

This may sounds like an unrealistically positive environment, but you'll know it's possible after reading this book. You'll have seen how each of the essential factors just mentioned is largely under the control of management and that none require rocket science for their provision. You'll understand why the P-7™ system has been used by thousands of managers, across the globe, to improve the performance of their staff, their project teams, their colleagues and their own performance.

None of the seven factors are esoteric, and none require technical finesse to use. At first glance, you maybe be tempted to say: "These factors are so simple…it's just common sense…we must already do this!" Pause for a moment to realize however: Common sense is not always common practice. This book makes it common practice to practice effective performance management—and, I believe, does it in a way that's easy to learn and simple to apply.

William E. Beane, Ph.D.
July, 2013
St. Louis, Missouri

Simplicity is the ultimate sophistication.
STEVE JOBS

CONTENTS

ACKNOWLEDGMENTS

This book would never have come to fruition without the caring encouragement, support and assistance of my wife, Diana. She read countless drafts and contributed innumerable suggestions that made the book better and more understandable. In addition, she endured all of the nights and weekends when "working on the book" took time away from her and my family.

The final editing was done by my longtime friend and colleague, Bill Chott. Bill is a supremely gifted writer and editor who shaped my wandering prose into a much more readable final form. His contribution has been invaluable. Final proofing was done by Renee Gunterman, who should consider writing, editing and proofing as a professional career.

I could recite a long list of colleagues, clients and users who, over the years, have proven the impact of the P-7™ system while they have also improved its application; but I know I would forget to mention some who were very helpful. In particular, I would like to thank Dennis Lettow, Jeff Johnson, Pat Gannon and Gary Winter for their support and contributions to P-7, as both clients and friends.

Finally, I would like to thank my clients and the thousands of managers, both domestic and global, for their ongoing use and helpful critique of the system over the past 15 years. For me, they came disguised as clients and end-users, but they were truly teachers.

TESTIMONIALS

"For many years, training in our organization was, too frequently, an overused solution to performance problems. We knew that analyzing performance was a better way; but training seemed easier and performance analysis involved complicated flow charts. When we learned about P-7, we knew we had found the simplest, most powerful management tool available. We've conducted P-7 problem-solving workshops for managers in 15 countries. and their feedback is virtually identical: "This is the most practical and helpful management tool I use.

"Not only can we pinpoint the problem causes, but we know what to do about it. To this day, managers who first learned about P-7 15 years ago still ask to have it for their new people. With this book, P-7 will become even more popular."

DENNIS J. LETTOW, SALES DEVELOPMENT DIRECTOR (RETIRED), DUPONT-PIONEER

"We need good employees!" That's the typical cry of supervisors.
MIND THE GAP explains the do-able actions management can perform to positively affect employees. employee achievements are very dependent on the application of the P-7 principles, which are at the disposal of our management. In my experience, the culture of the workplace is enhanced—and employee engagement is improved—as P-7 is applied."

JEFF JOHNSON, HEAD OF STRATEGY & GROWTH: DEALER CHANNEL, SYNGENTA

"Anyone with responsibility for the performance of others will discover that Mind the Gap is an excellent tool, conceived with the elegance of simplicity. This book's practical and logical method allows managers to exercise owner-ship and accountability by helping them clearly identify the gaps in per-formance issues. That enables them to drive positive change through people and processes."

MARTI CORTEZ, VICE PRESIDENT, QUALITY, PROCESS AND COMMUNICATIONS:
CHARTER COMMUNICATIONS

"During the more than 20 years that I have worked with Bill Beane, his focus has always been on improving the performance of others. In my experience, performance diagnosis and improvement is one of the most difficult tasks that managers face. Many just get frustrated; they ignore problems, or worse, resort to termination as the only answer. They may know WHY performance management is necessary; but they do not know WHAT is effective, or HOW to get increased performance or a positive change in behavior. The P-7 System not only supplies the structure needed to identify performance/behavioral issues; it also creates a written action plan to guide the process."

PATRICK J. GANNON. DIRECTOR OF TRAINING (RETIRED), BRUNSWICK CORPORATION

"One of the biggest challenges of today's managers is to get day-to-day work done while effectively managing the performance of his or her employees. No matter how objective we try to make the process of performance evaluation, it is still very subjective in nature. And managers, as well as HR professionals, lack the necessary tools and methodologies to deal with critical performance issues.

"I've been using the Performance-7 System for the past four years now and believe it should be included in every manager's' and HR professional's toolbox. With Performance-7, a manager can use the worksheets to effectively and consistently diagnose the "gap" of any performance issue, identify the source of the issue, and provide clear action steps to fully resolve the performance problem. It's simplicity is its strength!"

RICH ELDERKIN, GLOBAL OD AND TRAINING, BIO-RAD LABORATORIES

OVERVIEW

ALL TOO FAMILIAR?

If you manage and coordinate the work of others, you're virtually certain to be acquainted with issues like these:

- A team member is performing unevenly. Some parts of her job are going well, but other tasks consistently miss your expectations.

- A direct report has been chronically late with his work. You have repeatedly mentioned that, but his brief improvements soon slide back into old habits.

- A team or department you inherited is in disarray. The previous manager had assured everyone their performance was "great," when, in fact, the department's performance is fairly mediocre.

Even if you don't manage others directly, but instead work with them on projects, you've undoubtedly encountered issues like this:

- A peer simply isn't meeting his commitments on an important joint project. You're concerned that, because of his poor performance, the project may fail, making you both look bad.

- You've been given a project with ambiguous goals and objectives and been told to "do your best." This has happened before; and you feel that you've been set up to fail, even though the project is barely underway.

- You're working with colleagues in another division to get a new product released. Although meetings and deadlines are set, events are often delayed; and you don't get what you need on time. At some point, you sigh and ask:
  Why is it that the simple things I expect from others are so often fouled up? What's happening with our projects? Why do we seem to drop the ball so often around here?

1

EXECUTION: THE LIFE-FORCE OF EVERY ORGANIZATION

If the preceding scenarios seem all-too-familiar, realize you're not alone. Every day, in virtually every organization, little things—and sometimes big ones—fall through the cracks. Some of these execution issues are merely annoyances; others, however, can substantially impact your execution and business results.

They often become so prevalent that they become accepted as part of the fabric of "how we do things around here." Because we adapt to them, they can pour continuous sand in the gears of execution as we try to produce business results.

When performance is less than what was expected, execution always suffers. The great news is: Ineffective execution is a solvable problem. Once you learn the basic factors involved in effective performance, you equip yourself to quickly diagnose and fix problems such as:

- Lack of performance by a direct report or team member
- Inadequate support from colleagues and peers
- Team and/or organizational dysfunction
- Lack of performance support from your manager
- Poor performance by a task force or project team

A GLIMPSE AT WHAT'S AHEAD

Chapter 1: Introduction to the Performance-7™(P-7™) system for analyzing and improving performance problems—issues that sabotage effective execution.

Chapter 2: Prerequisite for using the system: Identifying the gap.

Chapter 3: First factor (P1) in the P-7 System, focusing on adequacy of task design. How a factor P1 (task) is then applied to a sample performance issue.

Chapter 4: Second factor (P2) in the P-7 System, focusing on clear, matching expectations. How factor P2 (expectations) is then applied to the same sample performance issue.

Chapter 5: Third factor (P3) in the P-7 System, focusing on performance feedback. How factor P3 (feedback) is then applied to the same sample performance issue.

Chapter 6: Fourth factor (P4) in the P-7 System, focusing on competence to perform. How factor P4 (competence) is then applied to the same sample performance issue.

Chapter 7: Fifth factor (P5) in the P-7 System, focusing on understanding task importance. How factor P5 (importance) is then applied to the same sample performance issue.

Chapter 8: Personal performance factors:

- Sixth factor (P6) in the P-7 System, focusing on both capability and willingness to perform. How the factors of P6, capability and willingness, are applied to a sample performance issue.

- Seventh and final factor (P7) in the P-7 System, focusing on personal issues. How factor P7 is applied to an ongoing performance issue. Demonstrate of the P-7 System performance worksheet. Discussion of how to interpret P7 answers.

Chapter 9: Summary of P-7 analysis. How to use the system to analyze and improve the collaboration from a peer—and the performance of a team, a department or an entire organization.

Chapter 10: How to extend the P-7 System to address peer or manager issues.

Chapter 11: Applications of P-7 for individual contributors: The P-7 Contract.

Chapter 12: How to apply the P-7 System to projects.

Chapter 13: Why it's critical to use the P-7 System.

Chapter 14: P-7 Analysis of a sample case performance management performance gap.

CHAPTER 1

INTRODUCTION TO PERFORMANCE-7™

The Performance-7™ (P-7™) Analysis and Improvement System was designed to be a tool for managers to analyze and improve performance by targeting the number 1 problem plaguing every business—ineffective execution. The system achieves that objective by identifying the factors essential for individuals to perform a given task.

Design of the system began by seeking answers to the question: *What basic factors must be in place for someone to perform a task successfully?* Answers to this question identified seven critical performance factors.

1. The **task** must be "do-able"—designed for success. You can't expect the impossible.

Performers have to:

2. Know what's expected; expectations have to be clear and unambiguous.
3. Be able to get feedback on their performance.
4. Know how to perform the task.
5. Understand why performance is important both for them and for the organization.
6. Be able and willing to perform the task as expected.
7. Have minimal outside interference from personal concerns and issues.

The system applies to varying situations; and the wording changes slightly as the system is applied differently. However, the seven factors remain as the constant requirements for performance across all situations.

ORIENTATION TO THE SYSTEM

The system is best understood by examining each of the seven factors individually.

P1 — Is the Task Designed for Success?

The task must be one that people can perform successfully.

"Task" is defined as any action—task, project, process, procedure, job, etc.—that a person needs to execute effectively. Tasks that are unrealistic (impossible to do successfully), poorly designed, or attempted without adequate resources cannot be executed successfully.

Task design (P1) is the first factor in the P-7 System because it's the only factor that has little or nothing to do with the task performer. You may know this intuitively from personal experience.

Recall a time when you were given an assignment with an unrealistic deadline . . . an outmoded, cumbersome process . . . inadequate resources. You probably felt: "I've been set up to fail before I get started." What effect did this situation have on your commitment and execution?

P2 — Are Expectations Clear and Matching?

People have to know what's expected.

Research in the field of performance clearly indicates that ambiguous, misaligned or missing expectations are the single most frequent cause of execution issues.

When expectations are vague or unclear, people attempt to "fill in the blanks" with what they think the expectations probably are or should be. This virtually ensures that performers will direct their efforts toward a set of expectations different from those intended—and that a failure to execute effectively is highly likely.

You probably can relate to this scenario:

> You're assigned a task with ambiguous expectations; you try to do your best, only to hear later: "That's not what you were supposed to be doing; you should have known what I needed."

Think back. What effect did that have on your commitment to, and execution of, the task?

P3 — Has Timely, Quality Feedback Been Given?

People have to know how well they're doing.

Feedback has two primary functions. It can either keep a task on track or put it back on track when it gets derailed.

When performance is on track, reinforcing feedback (praise, recognition and appreciation) helps motivate further good performance. It also confirms that performance is meeting the right expectations. Positive feedback, therefore, strengthens expectations.

In cases where performance isn't on track, corrective feedback helps performers improve their execution toward expectations. Without feedback, people assume that whatever they are doing must be "right." That false assumption invariably leads to misaligned expectations and execution failures.

Consider times when you felt you went "above and beyond" the call of duty, only to have no one notice or appreciate your efforts—or the times you pushed forward with no feedback, only to hear later: "What's wrong with you? This isn't what I wanted. You should have known to check in with me." What effect did that kind of outcome have on your commitment and execution?

P4 — Is the Person Competent to Perform Successfully?

People must have the knowledge and skills to do the task.

The P4 factor is the "training" factor. The good news about this factor is that it's subject to your control. The competence on which it focuses can be acquired or built. A person can learn how to program software . . . run a drill press . . . bake a cake.

The fact that competence can be acquired distinguishes it from capability which is innate and cannot be acquired. Capability falls under another factor that we discuss later.

The following scenario should give you a feel for the importance of the P4 factor.

You're a novice swimmer who still hasn't mastered treading water, but you've been put on a swimming team. The team captain announces that your first task is to get to the shallow end of the pool 20 yards away. He then suddenly throws you into the deep end, apologizing from poolside: "We don't have time for swimming lessons. We're too shorthanded." You flail about, swallowing gulps of water, fighting to keep your head above water.

How is this "training" going to affect your commitment and execution?

P5 — Does the Person Understand the Importance of the Task both Personally and to the Organization?

People have to be aware of just how important the task is.

Factor 5 addresses two issues: the personal importance of the task and its importance to the organization. If a person has little recognition of both the reward for performing well and the consequences of performing poorly, it's likely that performance will suffer.

The same is true of recognizing the importance of a task to the organization. Failure to grasp organizational significance translates to the person considering good performance unimportant. Envision a situation in which you're assigned a task to which no one seems to pay any attention and which doesn't appear to be very important. Next, ask yourself if you're motivated to give your best. Then, pose yourself another question: What's the resulting effect on your commitment and execution?

P6 — Is the Performer Capable and Willing to Perform the Task?

People must be able to, and be motivated to, perform the task successfully.

Like Factor 5, Factor 6 addresses two aspects of task performance: capability and willingness. The P-7 System addresses them simultaneously because both are internal attributes of the person.

The difference between Factor 6 (capability) and Factor 4 (competence) is that no one, the performer included, has much control over capability. Capability is innate talent—something that can't be learned.

Capability defined in P-7 terms is: The match between the physical, mental and emotional requirements of the task and the physical, mental and emotional limits of the performer. You've experienced being incapable of performing a task when you were in a situation where you felt you were "in over your head." When you felt like that, what effect did it have on your commitment and execution?

The willingness aspect of Factor 6 is fairly straightforward and presumed to be under the control of the performer. Revisit performing a task you didn't enjoy but still carried out as required to meet expectations. Were you reluctant to perform the task but then decided to "grin and bear it"—to perform well even though you disliked the task? What effect did your willingness have on your commitment and execution?

P7 – Can Personal Issues be Ruled Out as a Factor Affecting Performance?

Performers must have minimal interference from outside (personal) issues.

From time to time, almost everyone experiences transitory issues such as health problems, family crises, or other personal issues that can interfere with performance on the job. To see if such issues are performance obstacles, the Factor 6 question is framed so that a "yes" answer is a positive response.

If you've ever tried to stay focused at work while facing personal issues, you realize that such issues can be distracting or debilitating. Ask yourself what impact the issues you were facing had on your commitment to, and execution of, the task to which you were assigned.

SUMMARY

The P-7 System focuses on varying applications of seven key performance factors:

Whether a *task* is . . .

- "Do-able" – P1 (Chapter 3)

Whether a *performer* has . . .

- Clear, aligned and matching expectations – P2 (Chapter 4)
- Received timely, balanced and honest feedback – P3 (Chapter 5)
- Competence and know-how to perform the task – P4 (Chapter 6)
- Understanding of a task's importance, both for themselves and for the organization (What's In It For Them – WIIFT) – P5 (Chapter 7)

- Personal issues distracting from performance – P6 and P7 (Chapter 8)

Before applying the P-7 System factors, a preliminary step whose importance cannot be underestimated must be taken: the prerequisite step of identifying the gap.

CHAPTER 2

PREREQUISITE STEP: IDENTIFYING THE GAP

P-7 performance improvement begins by identifying the performance gap. The performance gap, as defined by the system, is the difference between the performance desired or needed (expected performance) and the performance actually observed or measured (actual performance). In the case of a currently good performer, the gap could be failing to realize the potential and top-notch contribution he or she could make if all performance factors were in place.

Although identifying the gap may seem to be a rather obvious, simple step, real-world experience has proven it's too important to skip. Failure to specify the gap up front often leads to lack of urgency in addressing the problem.

That indifference can result in an "Ain't that a shame" reaction—a Latent Voice Episode (LVE). More about that shortly. It's a situation in which a person may be frustrated—perhaps even angry—but continues to tolerate the problem, even while continuing to complain about it. When discussing performance problems with managers, we hear this "complaint with no action" refrain repeatedly.

The shortfall then becomes accepted as a part of the natural order of things and consequently doesn't go away. The person simply sighs and says, "Ain't that a shame." A greater shame is underestimating the importance of the P-7 initial gap identification step.

Identifying the gap has also been proven to lead to further analysis and increased improvement. It not only clarifies the gap; it directs the focus of the performance improvement process. What's more, defining the gap forces the implementer to specify expected performance and observe actual performance. This twofold action then supports performance analysis.

In the case of a top performer, we're not talking about a "gap" as much as an unrealized potential. The reason is that the individual doesn't have the factors necessary to unleash his or her full potential. Although our focus here is on performance issues, helping solid performers achieve their potential is always a management responsibility.

SAMPLE APPLICATION

The best way to illustrate the seven performance factors is to see how they're applied to a hypothetical situation. The following example illustrates how each of the seven factors is applied to a sample performance issue problem involving late or incomplete reports.

Scenario

Envision yourself as the manager of a direct report named Fred. Here, your thoughts betray your frustration:

Fred's dropped the ball again on the report I assigned him. So, here I go again, staying late to rewrite his report. I can't figure out what's wrong with Fred. But I know one thing for certain. I'm running out of patience with him.

Prerequisite Step

You decide to solve the problem using the Performance-7 System, starting with the all-important preparation step: Identifying the gap. The first action is to state your expected performance. You summarize it as follows:

"Fred should complete his assigned reports on time and with high quality, so I can pass them on to other team members without having to rework them."

You summarize actual performance this way:

"Fred's writing assignments are either late or poorly done; I often have to rewrite his reports before sharing them with others."

Note that the description of actual performance says nothing about: "what's wrong with Fred" or "I'm running out of patience." It's simply a clear description of the difference between expected and actual performance.

You have now identified the late/poor report gap.

APPLYING THE P-7 SYSTEM

Having identified the gap, you're ready to apply each of the seven P-7 factors to the gap. The following chapters illustrate how best to do that by continuing this sample case.

CHAPTER 3

P1: IS THE TASK DESIGNED FOR SUCCESS?

"Give me a motivated performer in a lousy process . . .
the process will win every time."
GEARY RUMMLER

People need performance tasks that can be done successfully. The P-7 System addresses task issues with P1, the first factor in the system.

Why tackle task design first? Because it's the only factor that has little or nothing to do with the performer. Logically, if task design is poor, then virtually any performer will struggle. If a person is trying to perform a task that's impossible, poorly designed, or lacking adequate resources, that person most likely will fail—or at least have diminished success.

TASK DESIGN

Three elements contribute to the task design factor:

1. Actual or perceived *realism*.
2. *Design* of the task, process or procedures.
3. Availability of *resources*.

Let's examine them one by one.

Is the Task Realistic?

If the task expectation is—or even just appears to be—unrealistic, even the most capable performers are unlikely to be successful. An example of an unrealistic expectation would be asking someone to complete a four-week job in four days. Others would be asking a person to multi-task several complex projects at once or closely manage a team of 55.

People often try their best to perform an unrealistic task; yet they're still virtually destined to fail. Realists may accurately sense the task as "undo-able" and simply go through the motions. The importance of task realism is underscored by the fact that so many managers have been taught over the years to set S.M.A.R.T. Goals, where the "R" in S.M.A.R.T. stands for "realistic."

It's important to distinguish between goals that are simply challenging or a stretch and those that are truly unrealistic. Effective managers often set goals that challenge their team. Managers who consistently set completely unrealistic goals, on the other hand, eventually lose not only their credibility but also the respect and trust of their people.

Is the Task Well Designed?

If you're looking for a great recipe for failure, ask people to perform a poorly designed task. That's simply a paraphrase of the quote from Geary Rummler that opened this chapter. Rummler is one of the founding fathers of performance improvement. He fully recognized that a poorly designed process or procedure will handicap even the most capable and willing performer.

No one sets out to beget a poorly designed task. Experience implementing the P-7 System, however, identified two "genes" as the source of task design problems. The genetic culprits are inattention and obsolescence.

Inattention: Design by Default

A task that suffers from benign neglect has been generated by what P-7 facilitators call "design by default." In a default design, no one pays much attention to a particular task, process or set of procedures. They just evolve over time, mutating on their own into a state so convoluted that no one could possibly execute them successfully.

Default design tasks are often put into action with little consideration of what someone actually has to crawl through, or hop over, to succeed. It's all too easy to endorse a process that represents an obstacle course, if you don't have to run the obstacles yourself.

Obsolescence: "The way we've always done it around here"

The task or process design was initially greeted by standing ovations awhile back. Since then, however, many aspects of the task have changed in response to the current reality. Still, things continue to get done . . . *". . . the way we've always done them around here."*

That complacent refrain is all too familiar in too many organizations. They forge ahead, replete with procedures that are outmoded and/or difficult to execute.

Task design issues are so common that we've given an often-used name to attempts at executing a defective process: *"workaround."* Such so-called "solutions" are particularly common in organizations where managers label employee concerns about task design as "griping" or "whining." Obsolescence issues therefore tend to go unaddressed instead of being recognized as legitimate concerns demanding attention and action.

Are Resources Adequate?

A task that's under-resourced will seldom see a successful completion. That's virtually self-evident. Who hasn't struggled with a task at one time or another while thinking:

I could do this so much better if only I had the right tools or better equipment . . . time to concentrate . . . consistent support . . . enough hands on deck.

Too-lean staffing often breeds such frustration.

One example is a typical situation in which a team of three now struggles to complete the work formerly performed by a staff of five. The team may complete the task-but at what cost: sacrifice in quality . . . employee burnout?

Poor physical working conditions can also fall under the umbrella of inadequate resources. For example, the success of a complex task can very well be compromised by a noisy work environment. Inter-ruptions and distractions also earn minus signs in the formula for successful task completion.

SHORTCUT TO THE ANSWER

A quick way to help answer the P1 question of whether or not a task is designed for success is to determine if others have completed the same task successfully. A track record of success by others suggests that the task is "do-able"—and therefore that task design is probably not the cause of the gap.

Use caution in accepting this conclusion, however. Just because someone manages to muddle through a poorly designed task with some degree of success doesn't mean that the task design shouldn't be improved. Most people try hard to succeed, even when poor task design forces them to hurdle obstacles on the way to the finish line.

Before reaching a conclusion, make sure that people aren't using workarounds. Performers often do to make an unwieldy process work, long before they raise an issue or complain to management.

P1 SUMMARY

The key points to keep in mind in assessing whether or not a task is designed for success are:

- Task design is first on the P-7 list because it's unrelated to the performer. Get it wrong, and attempts to execute usually fail regardless of the skill of the performer.
- Task design has to meet three criteria: Realism, Design and Resources (RDR).
- All three factors of task design—RDR—are adequate to give a "yes" answer to the question: "Is this task designed for success?" If a task is poorly designed, execution is dead on arrival.
- If others routinely perform the task successfully, then task design is probably not a major cause of the gap.

SAMPLE APPLICATION

Assessment

Let's find out if there's a shortcut answer to the P1 issue of Fred's report writing tasks. His tasks are very similar to those being performed successfully by fellow team member.

In addition, there do not appear to be any resource or environmental issues affecting Fred. He uses the same resources, has the same deadlines, and his reports are no more complex than those of his teammates. Also, his tasks seem to have realistic expectations; and they are fairly well designed and properly resourced.

Conclusion

We can therefore subject Fred's case to the P1 test as follows:

PERFORMANCE FACTOR	Yes	No

P1 Is this task designed for success?
   • Are *others* performing this task well?
   • Is it *realistic*, well *designed*?
   • Are adequate *resources* committed to it?
	√	_

The "yes" answer to this question means that the task is probably not a cause of the problem. A "no" answer would have meant that that there were issues in task design that needed to be addressed.

If you were uncertain of the answer or knew that task execution had issues, then the next step would be to identify possible constraints by talking with Fred and/or his colleagues.

The people who perform a task are always the most knowledgeable about what's keeping the task from being optimally successful. You'll be surprised at how much information you can uncover by simply asking: "What's keeping you from being able to do this job more effectively?"

Honest attempts like this to surface negative issues are the way to unearth workarounds and discover frustrations people are experiencing in performing the task. So, don't give the P1 question a "yes" answer too quickly just because you are unaware of task issues others are dealing with. It may be that people have just been waiting for you to ask.

"Why don't they just speak up," you wonder? The answer comes from researchers examining this question who identified fear as a major block to sharing task issues. They call the reluctance to speak up a Latent Voice Episode (LVE). An LVE is defined as:

> *"Those moments at work when someone considers speaking up, but it doesn't occur."*
> EDMONDSON AND DETERT (2005)

Unfortunately, LVEs occur quite often. The researchers indicated that the frequency of this self-censorship is almost 70% when the issue is related to changes or improvements needed in the workplace.

More senior or more secure employees are more likely to share issues rather freely. However, many rank-and-file employees see the safest bet as: Keep your thoughts to yourself, unless you're asked.

> *"If you can't describe what you're doing as a process,*
> *you don't know what you're doing."*
>
> W. EDWARDS DEMING

NEXT . . . P2: CLEAR, MATCHING EXPECTATIONS

Having a task that can be performed successfully is a good start toward improving performance. However, there are six more factors necessary to ensure successful performance—knowing exactly what performance is expected, for example.

Performance expectations are linked with task design in that unrealistic expectations make any task, almost by definition, "undo-able." The next chapter, focusing on the P2 factor of the P-7 System, examines whether or not expectations, as understood by the performer, are clear—and if they match the expectations of the organization or manager assigning the task.

CHAPTER 4

P2: ARE EXPECTATIONS CLEAR AND MATCHING?

"It ain't what we don't know that hurts us . . .
It's what we know, that ain't so."
WILL ROGERS

There's no question about the overriding importance of the second P-7 System question. Both research data and the collective observation of virtually all of my performance clients over the years have validated this fact: Having unclear, mismatched or missing expectations is the single most common cause of performance issues.

WHAT'S AN EXPECTATION?

Like most managers, you may be scratching your head right now asking: "How in the world can this be happening? Especially after all the emphasis we placed on setting SMART goals . . . having clear expectations . . . setting quarterly targets. How could something so simple and basic be such a big problem?"

The answer begins with the concept of "expectations" itself. he concept lends itself to often being vague. Expectations can be as immediate and focused as:

The three specific things you need to finish this afternoon are . . .
Or as broad as:
Our five-year revenue goals include annual growth of 15%."

An expectation can be:

As brief as an emotional charge to "Sell 10% more than last year."
Or
As definitive as a complex task performance standard outlining technical qualitative and quantitative requirements for a part or a process.

The list goes on.

Expectations sometimes refer only to outcomes such as quotas or targets: "Sell at least $5,000 of merchandise per week." Some end at that. Others, because of the situation and maturity of the performer, may also outline the methods, procedures and activities to be used in achieving those outcomes: "To meet your sales quota, we expect you to make 25 cold calls per week."

THE "SHOULD" DEFENSE

The P-7 team has isolated one of the biggest barriers to clear, matching expectations. It's a simple, single word: "should." Managers use it frequently to shield themselves from blame for performance shortfalls. Witness:

"Sara's been here long enough. She should know what I want."
"Tom, you're a professional You should know what we need from you without having to ask."

"Should" becomes the defense for a multitude of assumptions. A typical example:

"They should know what I want, so I assume they do know what I want; therefore, I don't have to tell them any more."

It's not hard to see where the "should" defense can lead. It can cast blame on a person for not correctly guessing our true expectations. It can find a person guilty of lacking telepathic ability.

MISPERCEPTIONS LEAD TO MISSED EXPECTATIONS

The "should" defense gets people's attention because it's not totally unfounded. Every performer does, in fact, have at least a vague idea of what's required from them on the the job. No one operates without performance expectations. The question is: Where did those expectations come from?

Expectations have numerous sources: the boss, coworkers, sometimes an active imagination. They may even come from testing the waters and waiting for feedback. It's worth the effort to tap your personal experiences to see where some of yours came from in the past.

Think back to a time when you moved on to a new job or undertook a different set of responsibilities and felt you didn't fully understand what was expected of you. What did you do to construct a clearer picture of your job expectations? If you're like most of us, you observed what others with similar tasks or responsibilities were trying to accomplish, then modeled their activities as a way of trying to meet expectations.

Another approach may have been taking your best shot at self-defining expectations, then waiting for reactions. If you didn't receive any performance feedback, you breathed a sigh of relief for having guessed correctly. You took comfort from the classic organizational adage:

> *"You'll hear from the boss if there's a problem. Otherwise things are OK."*

When managers learn how prevalent misperceptions can be, they typically respond: "Well . . . why don't people just step forward and ask for clarification if they don't know what's expected?" They've forgotten how they thought when they occupied a lower rung on the organizational ladder.

People typically don't want to admit, or hear, that they must not have been listening closely enough . . . that they have failed to comprehend the obvious. In most corporate cultures, asking the boss for clarification is one of the last things most line employees would think of doing.

Everyone fears losing face or credibility—or being labeled a "complainer." The solution for many people is the silent treatment.

"YES" PEOPLE

This same mentality that underlies the silent treatment typically exists when a person's manager asks the closed question: "Do you know what's expected on this job?" The manager usually could have saved their breath. The invariable answer is a self-protective, "yes."

Another kind of "yes" person gives their affirmative response, not out of face-saving behavior, but as the result of a far deeper problem. They actually think they understand expectations . . . even though they don't.

How could someone who reports to you arrive at such a misconception? Almost surely because you haven't told them otherwise! They feel that since they haven't heard anything from you about missing expectations, they must be on target.

Case in point:

1. Tanya's boss assumes Tanya knows what's expected.
2. Tanya thinks she does know what's expected.
3. Neither Tanya nor her boss see any need to discuss expectations.

RESULT: Expectations remain unclear; the problem persists, particularly in the absence of regular feedback.

Experience in P-7 implementation clearly singles out mismatched, ambiguous or missing expectations as the single performance factor most responsible for ineffective execution. A negative response to the P2 question is therefore definitely the 1000-pound gorilla of execution problems.

P2 problems call for urgent corporate attention, especially considering that this type of mismatch occurs frequently, across every level of virtually every company. The cost of not having clear, matching expectations in terms of ineffective execution is therefore quite significant.

P2 SUMMARY

The key points to remember about the P2 factor are:

- Lack of clear, matching expectations is the most frequent cause of performance gaps across organizations.
- Even when people are uncertain about expectations, they seldom ask for clarification because they don't want to lose face.
- Sometimes both managers and direct reports mistakenly think they have a shared, mutual understanding of expectations.
- Everyone has a picture of what is expected of them on the job. If managers don't paint a full canvas, people fill in the blanks.
- Lack of clear expectations also sends the unintentional message that a particular expectation is not an important priority.

SAMPLE APPLICATION
Assessment

Let's focus on the effect P2 issues may have on Fred. You haven't always given Fred consistent expectations on timeliness and haven't been very specific about issues of report quality. You've basically just told Fred to "do a better job."

Conclusion

You need to clarify the requirements. You therefore must answer question P2 "no" since it's uncertain that expectations are clear.

PERFORMANCE FACTOR	Yes	No
P2 Are expectations clear and matching? • Are expectations and standards certain to be fully understood? • Do expectations/priorities match?	—	√

NEXT . . . P3: HAS TIMELY, QUALITY FEEDBACK BEEN GIVEN?

The following chapter examines the second-most-important factor in effective performance: Feedback.

CHAPTER 5

P3: HAS TIMELY, QUALITY FEEDBACK BEEN GIVEN?

"Feedback . . . the breakfast of champions."
ANONYMOUS

Every manager can recite the importance of providing regular feedback and reinforcing good performance. That doesn't mean it happens, however. Most 360-feedback and employee surveys indicate that when it comes to giving constructive feedback, our hearts may be in the right place, but our habits often aren't.

Such bad habits exacerbate performance problems because P2 expectations and P3 feedback are strongly intertwined. When one is missing, often the other is, too. What's more, performance research shows that neither expectations nor feedback alone has the same impact in supporting high performance as do both together.

It makes sense, therefore, that when expectations (P2) are vague or missing, feedback (P3) will also be less than adequate. Otherwise, feedback could sound something like:

"Why haven't you done what I haven't told you I needed you to do?"

Most managers know it would be ridiculous to make such a statement. So, when they realize that they haven't given clear expectations, they're likely to also avoid giving focused feedback.

TWO VITAL FUNCTIONS OF FEEDBACK

When feedback is missing, performance is obviously impaired. The damage occurs because the two vital functions of feedback are missing: reinforcement of good performance (positive feedback) and keeping people on track (constructive feedback).

Positive Feedback

Positive feedback reinforces good performance and clarifies expectations. Praise and recognition are examples of feedback for a job well done. They enable people to take pride in their work and support continued high performance.

Both elements are critical in building motivation and high engagement. Their impact is addressed on later pages.

Constructive Feedback

Constructive feedback not only keeps people on track, helping nudge them back on course when they go astray, it also clarifies the correct expectations. Conversely, lack of constructive feedback allows performers to stray further off track, lowering results even more—and sends the unintentional message: "Whatever you're doing is OK."

Hearing silence rather than constructive feedback assures people that their performance is fine. From our first job on, we've been told that we'll hear from our manager if there's a problem. No news is good news.

Impact of No Feedback

Lack of either clear matching expectations (P2) or timely, constructive feedback (P3) is bad enough; but consider the overall impact on performance when both are missing. Get ready for a real train wreck!

P-7 research indicates that employees feel expectations are lacking 62 percent of the time and that feedback is inadequate 57 percent of the time. That certainly explains why organizations are constantly experiencing performance problems.

Another equally insidious outcome of failure to give feedback is that employees begin to make assumptions—for example:

"No one is paying any attention."

OR WORSE

"What I'm doing can't be all that important."

No one gets excited about performing an "unimportant" task. In Chapter 7 on P5 task understanding, you'll see how a person's motivation to do their best drops off quickly when they perceive a task to be unimportant or irrelevant.

"Should" – A Recurring Role

As with expectations, the word "should" also plays a role in feedback Managers typically feel that team members *should* know that they're doing okay . . . *should* know how the manager feels about their performance . . . *should* be able to soldier-on without appreciation.

Assumption again raises its ugly head. Here, it substitutes for clear communication on performance.

OPTIMAL FEEDBACK

For feedback to be optimal in supporting performance, it must meet four standards. Optimal feedback is:

- Timely
- Balanced
- Constructive
- Honest

Timely

Learning theory says that, as the gap between a behavior and feedback on that behavior increases, the feedback rapidly becomes less relevant and effective. Why is it, then, that in many companies, delayed feedback seems to be the rule, rather than the exception?

During performance workshops, our P-7 team often asks: "How many of you receive most of your performance feedback once a year or even less often?" Almost always, most of the people in the room raise their hands. It's quite dismaying.

Performance management isn't something to be done once a year—or even semi-annually. It ought to be a continuous process. And responsibility for doing that lies with the leader.

In addition to learning theory's lesson that the impact of feedback erodes quickly if there's a significant gap between occasions on which it it is given, there's an additional adverse consequence. Ineffective performance has been allowed to continue during the gap between identifying a problem and addressing it. Ineffective performance, in other words, has real costs.

Balanced

Effective feedback tells both what's working well and what isn't. There's a balance between the two. One isn't emphasized more than the other.

Also, performers have no question about where they stand. That's not the case if feedback tilts too much to one side or the other.

When feedback is skewed to the negative side, performers may feel that they are being singled out, picked on, or treated unfairly. Their self confidence and morale can be shaken.

Conversely, a steady diet of only positive feedback sends the message that no improvement is necessary—maybe not even possible. Performers can develop a false sense of accomplishment and complacency which could be obstacles to their going from good to great.

Balanced feedback is honest. It helps clarify the parameters of expectations and priorities.

Constructive

Constructive feedback is information that helps people improve their performance. It doesn't merely criticize.

Coaching can also accompany constructive feedback when appropriate. Such coaching helps performers stay on track, or get back on track, with their performance.

Honest

Effective feedback is candid. Therefore, it's delivered with honesty and respect. Never is it judgmental, demeaning or shaming. Nor does it ever convey an inflated sense of accomplishment.

MANAGEMENT FEEDBACK BEHAVIOR

"My boss is tough but fair." When someone describes their boss like that, they're talking about a boss whose feedback behavior reflects all four standards of optimal feedback.

Effective feedback holds others accountable, while helping them improve. Its goal is always successful performance. P2 and P3, clear expectations and feedback, are unquestionably the two most powerful high-performance factors.

P3 SUMMARY

The key points to take away concerning the P3 factor are:

- Feedback can be either positive or constructive.
- Positive feedback is motivating and helps clarify expectations.
- Constructive feedback gets performance back on track while also clarifying expectations.
- When people don't get feedback, they give themselves feedback, which is often "I'm doing OK." Although this maintains self esteem, it may also reinforce mistaken expectations or priorities.

Performers need both clear, matching expectations and quality feedback to maximize their performance. If either is missing, performance usually suffers. If both are missing, an execution disaster certainly looms.

"Should" thinking again clouds the issue, as in:

*"They **should** know how they're doing."*
   OR
*"They **should** know what I think about their performance."*

SAMPLE APPLICATION

Assessment

You've griped at Fred now and then about both timeliness and quality, but haven't identified specific report quality issues.

Conclusion

You need to answer P3 as "no."

PERFORMANCE FACTOR	Yes	No
P3 Has quality feedback been given: timely, constructive, balanced and honest? • Was feedback *positive* to motivate and reinforce expectations? • Was feedback *constructive* to get the person back on track and clarify expectations?	—	√

NEXT . . . P4: COMPETENCE TO PERFORM WITH SKILLS & KNOWLEDGE

The following chapter illustrates how improving performance includes ensuring a performer actually knows how to perform an assigned task. A well designed task, clear expectations, and good feedback aren't enough.

CHAPTER 6

P4: DOES THE PERFORMER HAVE THE COMPETENCE (SKILLS AND KNOWLEDGE)?

"An empowered organization is one in which individuals have the knowledge, skill, desire, and opportunity to personally succeed."
STEPHEN R. COVEY

Stephen Covey is referring to the "training" factor in the P-7 System: Does the person have the required competence—skills, knowledge and/or experience—to perform the task successfully? If not, there's good news: Competence can be acquired. A person can learn how to program software, analyze a financial statement, bake a cake.

Much of the skill and knowledge a person gains comes either from experience on the job or other more formal training and development experiences labeled as "accelerated experience." No matter how it's acquired, the competence a person gains allows that person to perform successfully.

COMPETENCE VS. CAPABILITY

It's important to distinguish between competence, which can be acquired, and capability or talent. Capability is innate; it comes from within the individual. (A further discussion of capability appears in the Chapter 8 discussion of Factor P6.)

Ensuring that people perform successfully is a basic and essential management responsibility. It's therefore critical that managers be able to distinguish between issues of competence and issues of capability.

Both competence and capability can result in performance gaps that look similar. As a rule of thumb, if you've made legitimate and adequate efforts to build a person's competence, but the person is still struggling with the task, the problem is more likely capability than competence.

Diagnosis that a performer lacks the capability to perform a task rather than the competence is significant because we have little or no ability to change capability. A person who lacks capability will never be able to perform the task successfully.

That leaves only two possibilities: Assign the person to a different task, or make substantial changes to the task. Such a step has obvious impact on a performer's future career prospects, so the decision that a person lacks capability shouldn't be made lightly. P-7 experience shows that competence is a problem far more often than capability.

COSTS OF INCOMPETENCE

Identifying a problem, however, certainly doesn't solve it. Deciding a person needs competence doesn't insure the person gets the training and development they need to perform successfully. For example, in a crisis, employees are often thrust into the job with inadequate skills and knowledge and told: "Do your best" or "Watch what Simon does."

There's a price to be paid for such expediency. Performers typically struggle trying to learn a new task. Mistakes, foul-ups and frustration are to be expected. Costs mount up from lowered self-confidence, morale and, of course, ineffectiveness in getting the job done.

If task performance is critical or has direct impact on customers, the costs are ever greater. It's sadly not uncommon to find inadequately trained people bumbling through customer-facing tasks.

Customer service jobs are often low-wage positions involving mundane assignments. So, as might be expected, issues of competency often abound. Few and far between, unfortunately, are organizations that ensure employees in service positions are competent and well trained.

INCREASING COMPETENCE

The first step toward increasing competence should be determining whether or not competence is at a level that ensures successful task performance. That means doing a thorough analysis of the performer's training and development history in performing the task. If competence needs to be developed, then a plan outlining the requisite education, training, coaching and developmental activities needs to be developed to close the gap.

Competence and capability are actually somewhat intertwined. If the performer is capable of eventually learning how to perform well, but the learning curve is simply too slow for the demands of the job, the issue is twofold: competence and capability. The performer is incapable of gaining the necessary competence within a time frame necessary to get the job done.

P4 SUMMARY

The key points to remember about the P4 factor are:

- Competence (skills and knowledge to perform) can be acquired through training, development and experience.
- Competence can be acquired, unlike capability which depends on innate ability or talent.
- If adequate training and development have been provided and a gap remains, the issue is more likely one of capability rather than competence.
- Deciding that the gap is due to issues of capability rather than competence can have serious ramifications for the performer. Therefore, such decision should be made very carefully.

SAMPLE APPLICATION

Assessment

You're concerned that Fred may not know all of the key elements and structure necessary to write a good report.

Conclusion

Your P4 answer is "no."

PERFORMANCE FACTOR	Yes	No
P4 Does the performer have the competence to perform the task to expectations? ■ Does the performer have the *skills?* ■ Does the performer have the *knowledge and experience?*	—	√

NEXT . . . P5: UNDERSTANDING THE IMPORTANCE OF THE TASK

The topic of the next chapter is understanding task importance. This factor has significant impact on the motivation and commitment to perform.

CHAPTER 7

P5: DOES THE PERFORMER UNDERSTAND THE IMPORTANCE OF THE TASK?

"Success is going from failure to failure without a loss of enthusiasm."
WINSTON CHURCHILL

The fifth step of the P-7 Performance Improvement System focuses on ensuring that performers understand the importance of the task at two levels: personal importance to the performer and overall importance of the task to the organization. Both are necessary for successful performance.

PERSONAL IMPORTANCE OF THE TASK

A performer understands the personal importance of a task when he or she individually recognizes both:

- Gains, rewards or benefits—what's in it for me (WIIFM)— for performing a task well.
- Costs or consequences—what's not in it for me (WNIIFM)— of poor performance.

The P5 factor, along with positive feedback (P3), both emphasize the role motivation plays in the P-7 System. Understanding the personal benefits and costs of performance builds motivation to perform a task and gains commitment to performing the task effectively.

ASSESSING UNDERSTANDING OF IMPORTANCE

P5 poses three questions designed to assess understanding of personal importance (WIIFM):

1. Is there a personal gain for effective performance?
2. Are there personal consequences for poor performance?
3. Are there personal costs for good performance?

Much has been written and said about the importance of employee motivation. Nevertheless, the consequences of these highly personal factors are still too often overlooked.

1. Is There a Personal Gain for Effective Performance (WIIFM)?

Unless performers are rewarded through a strong pay-for-performance plan or commission system, most don't focus on monetary gain to answer the first assessment question. Instead, they typically ask their own questions—typically, *Does anybody here . . .*

- *Notice what I'm doing?*
- *Care about what I'm doing?*
- *Appreciate or recognize what I'm doing?*

These questions illustrate how strongly the element of P5 links with P3— feedback. Nothing motivates high performance more powerfully (and costs less to use) than positive feedback: focused praise, recognition and appreciation.

2. Are There Personal Consequences for Poor Performance (WNIIFM)?

The direct effects of there being no consequences for poor performance are very obvious: The performance gap becomes entrenched; the organization and its customers continue to pay the price.

When there are no consequences for poor performance, performers may feel that their current performance is "good enough." Even more damaging, lack of consequences signals an implied lack of task importance.

Combine a failure to hold people accountable for poor performance with neglect to recognize good performance, and you unleash an insidious force that devastates personal motivation. That twofold mistake also contaminates the second element of P5: organizational importance.

For performers, the logic is all too simple They conclude: "If doing this job right doesn't seem all that important to my boss, then how important can this job be?"

The secondary effects of ignoring task importance can result in even more devastation. When poor performance is ignored rather than being confronted—or worse, when good and bad performance are equally rewarded—you send a clear, loud, unmistakable, but unintentional, message: "Mediocre performance is OK."

Think about the impact your message has on other employees. Picture the impact it might have on your top "A" performers—team members you count on to always do the job to the best of their ability.

3. Are There Personal Costs for Good Performance (WNIIFM)?

"Personal consequences for doing the job well . . . how could that be?" you ask. Unfortunately, it can, and does, happen. Managers and co-workers do it all the time. They succeed in doing the one thing worse than failing to reward good performance: They punish it.

See if the following scenario rings a bell. It features the manager's go-to person, Jill. An "A" performer like most go-to people, she's typically rewarded for her superior performance by being awarded more work.

Today is no exception. Jill's manager runs her down as she heads out for lunch:

Jill . . . just got some last-minute input on the XYZ project. Has to be finished before my 1:00 p.m. meeting. Know I can count on you to deliver. Drop by my office when you're done so we can review. Thanks.

Combine continuing scenarios like this with a lack of appreciation. Then ask yourself why top performers often burn out or leave the company for greener pastures.

Superior performance can also draw a penalty in some militant union environments. Top performers are often cautioned by their peers against being a "rate-buster." Colleagues looking for overtime pay also remind top performers that there can be social costs for "getting too much done" during the regular work shift if overtime is reduced.

IMPORTANCE OF THE TASK TO THE ORGANIZATION

The second element of P5 focuses on the broader importance of the task to the organization—and by extension, to its customers. If a performer perceives how meaningful and important their task is to the organization, that perception has a strong impact on the person's motivation and the pride they feel for making a significant contribution.

Understanding organizational importance means that the performer sees the fit, value and contribution of their task to the organization and its customers. They perceive how their efforts support a flow, downstream to the customer.

Managers can ensure that employees understand organizational importance by communicating three concepts:

- Why the task is important.
- Where the task fits in the organization's processes.
- How the task contributes to the firm and links to value for customers.

Unfortunately, managers are typically better at telling people *what* needs to be done than they are at explaining *why* it's important. The *why*, however, is what really makes the commitment difference.

Research from the Gallup organization reflects why it's so critical to communicate task importance. They found that the majority of line employees, particularly those in lower-level positions, seldom appreciate the importance of their workday tasks.

This void of understanding robs them of the motivation and commitment to perform at their best. They miss out on the all-important sense of satisfaction and pride that comes from doing an important task well.

Organizational task importance and the accompanying motivation can be improved by letting people know and reminding them:

- How their job contributes to the bigger picture.
- That the importance of a task doesn't arise from its complexity or sophistication—that mundane tasks are also relevant and mission critical.

A special target group that needs to hear about the importance of their jobs are employees who aren't customer-facing. They often have no clear line of sight between what they do and what occurs downstream—or, ultimately, of their impact on customers and end users. Good managers supply this connection.

P5 SUMMARY

Keep these key points in mind when assessing the P5 factor:

- Task importance is both personal (what's in it, or not in it, for me) and organizational (why doing this task is important in the big picture). Both must be present to answer P5 with a "yes."

- Since the personal and organizational importance factors of P5 are interrelated, a problem in one negatively impacts the other.

- Personal task importance (gains, costs or punishments for performance) is a critical factor in determining commitment and engagement.

- Understanding the importance of a task requires understanding: the task's impact on others, what happens downstream, what happens to customers, and what happens when the task isn't performed well.

SAMPLE APPLICATION

Assessment

You feel that Fred sees the benefits of doing his reports well, but that he may not realize how much his lateness in delivering them is affecting his next performance review—or of the problems he causes for you and his coworkers when his work is late, or not up to expectations.

Conclusion

Because of your assessment, you have to answer the P5 question "no."

PROGRESS CHECK

The chart on the next page reviews your analysis to date and summarizes the meaning of the answers to P1 through P5.

PERFORMANCE FACTOR	Yes	No
P1 Is this task designed for success? • Are others performing this task well? • Is it *realistic*, well *designed*? • Are adequate *resources* committed to it?	√	—
P2 Are expectations clear and matching? • Are expectations and standards certain to be fully understood? • Do expectations/priorities match?	—	√
P3 Has quality feedback been given: timely, constructive, balanced and honest? • Was feedback *positive* to motivate and reinforce expectations? • Was feedback *constructive* to get the person back on track and clarify expectations?	—	√
P4 Does the performer have the competence to perform the task to expectations? • Does the performer have the *skills?* • Does the performer have the *knowledge and experience*?	—	√
P5 Does the performer understand the importance of the task personally and to the organization? • Does the performer realize the gains/costs of good/poor performance (WIIFM and WNIIFM)? • Does the performer know the importance of the task to the organization and customers?	—	√

Note that your P1 answer is the only "yes." You had problems with expectations, competence and task understanding which required you to answer "no."

The criteria are strict. Unless you can answer with an unequivocal "yes," your answer must be "no." Performance is diminished, regardless of the personal capability of the performer.

To state the obvious: As your thinking shifts from performance analysis to performance improvement, much of your focus needs to be on ensuring that every "no" answer to a question is changed to a resounding "yes." That's how the P-7 System not only helps analyze performance, but also provides direction toward plans for performance improvement. As you understand what could be causing the gap, you also see how to begin closing it.

The first five P-7 factors are called "success factors" because they're the essential elements for success, regardless of the performer. Problems in any of these five factors result in diminished performance, no matter what.

NEXT . . . P6 AND P7: THE PERSONAL PERFORMANCE FACTORS

The first five factors are more external to the performer. The final two P-7 factors are more closely related to the performer and are therefore designated as the personal performance factors.

CHAPTER 8

PERSONAL PERFORMANCE FACTORS:
CAPABILITY/WILLINGNESS, INTERFERING PERSONAL ISSUES

P6: IS THE PERFORMER CAPABLE AND WILLING TO PERFORM TO EXPECTATIONS?

"Executives owe it to the organization and to their fellow workers not to tolerate nonperforming individuals in important jobs."
PETER DRUCKER

Like P5, P6 is another dual-factor question. The two elements that P6 deals with are capability and willingness.

It's important to keep in mind the very different definitions the P-7 System gives competence and capability. This is in contrast to some performance models that combine them under the umbrella of "overall capability."

Capability Defined

When assessing any performer on any task, it's critical to distinguish between competence, which can be acquired, and capability, which is innate, like talent. One way to keep them straight is to think of capability as being "nature" and competence as being "nurture."

We can do little or nothing to change innate talents and capabilities. For example, although we can teach someone how to program a computer, we can't teach or coach them to be taller, or brighter or more stable.

Defined technically, capability is:

The fit between the mental, physical and emotional abilities of the performer compared to the mental, physical and emotional requirements of the task.

In other words, capability is what you bring to the party. It's like talent; it can't be injected or acquired, as is the case with competence. Marcus Buckingham and the Gallup researchers said it well when discussing management's role in dealing with capability or talent:

"People don't change that much. Don't waste time trying to put in what was left out. Try to draw out what was left in…that is hard enough."

When we put someone into a task that they can't handle well, we've made two mistakes: 1) We've mismatched capability against task requirements, which will definitely lower performance and raise frustration; and 2) we've also missed the opportunity to capitalize on that individual's strengths.

Years ago, Peter Drucker advised managers: *"Manage to peoples' strengths!"* How much time, money and human potential have been wasted by focusing on weaknesses! How much effort has been devoted to attempting to make "a silk purse from a cow's ear" instead of applying the strengths of the cow's ear to a more aligned task?

Incapability Explained

Why do we sometimes find a person assigned to a task, or placed in a job, that they are plainly incapable of handling? There are several possibilities.

Years ago, the late Laurence J. Peter introduced us to the "Peter Principle": People tend to get promoted until they reach a position that they are no longer capable of handling. The Peter Principle is still alive and well in many companies.

The wrong person in the wrong job can also be the result of a poor hiring or placement decision. Or a task may have grown so complex, or requirements may have grown so greatly, that it now takes a higher level of capability to handle them.

Whatever the reason, lack of capability or talent-fit can be the cause of any performance gap. That's bad enough. What's worse is compounding that error by putting someone in a job they can't handle, then leaving them there.

Willingness Defined

Willingness is even easier to define than capability. If often goes by different names: motivation, commitment, initiative, work ethics, ambition, effort, values. But it always boils down to just one thing: whether or not the performer is willing to perform the task to our expectations.

Moralistic or ethical judgments aside, willingness simply means whether or not a person is willing to do what a job or task requires. Virtually all of us have seen instances of someone simply not wanting to do what the job requires. That doesn't mean the person is bad. But it does mean their performance will almost always interfere with the execution we require.

Capability/Willingness Missing – Change Required

If either capability or willingness is impaired, task performance will invariably suffer. So, in either case, the manager needs to make a change involving the performer.

If *capability* is the issue—and the person is a willing worker—it makes sense for the manager to conclude:

- This person is in the wrong job.
- I need to find a task or job that better fits their talents and capabilities.

If the issue is *willingness*, the manager can logically conclude:

- We've probably made a poor hire.
- We need to start the ball rolling toward terminating the performer.

Unfortunately, that often isn't what happens with unwilling performers. They're often just transferred to another area or department, where they again have similar performance gaps. It's easier than confronting the issue and making the tough call.

Decision-making Cautions

As was the case with capability, a conclusion that willingness is the crux of the issue should be made carefully and deliberately. The primary reason is that such a conclusion can have significant consequences for the performer.

Also, lack of willingness isn't always solely the fault of the performer. Several other performance factors could be in play.

Factors Affecting Willingness

When facing an unrealistic or ambiguous task, employees may well feel less willing to engage and give their best. Problems with task understanding (P5) can also have a powerful negative impact on willingness.

Employees have to see a reason—a gain—for onerous tasks. Otherwise, their enthusiasm is likely to erode quickly.

Alternatives to Drastic Action

Reluctance to initiate the termination process should be the rule, not only because such an event has powerful negative ramifications for an employee's future career, but also because there may be a viable alternative. Implementation of sound, professional HR practices can usually screen out most incapable or unwilling applicants for positions.

Too many companies simply strap some wheels on their "C performers" and roll them around from department to department, rather than adopting a position of "up or out." Of course, dealing with willingness issues requires following your company's procedures for discipline and termination, so proper documentation and counsel with your HR group is important.

Special Cautions

Keep two very important cautions foremost in your mind as you prepare to answer Question P6:

1. Make certain that you've fully answered all five of the previous P-7 System questions-and that *no elements are missing from the analysis* leading to your P1 through P5 answers.

   Unless you cover all the bases, you can't get a reliable P6 answer. Elements missing in P1 through P5 performance analysis can result in misidentifying performance problems that merely look like those caused by capability or willingness issues. On the surface, they can appear to be identical.

2. Because of the career damage that can be done by labeling a person incapable of, or unwilling to do, a task, *be very careful about answering P6 "no."* Bring in your HR department early on in the process if you seem to be headed toward a "no."

P6 Summary

To summarize the P6 factor:

- Capability is innate and distinctly different from competence, which can be acquired.

- If a performer appears to be willing, but incapable, the best solution is to find them a job they can handle.

- Beware of making a mistake worse than putting a person into a job they can't handle: Leaving them there . . . struggling and failing.

- If willingness is certainly the issue, the best move is to cut your losses and start the termination process. Seldom does a performer who is unwilling in one context become highly willing in another.

- It's virtually impossible to answer P6 if anything is missing in P1 through P5. It's definitely impossible to answer P6 "no" in this instance because capability and willingness issues can't be distinguished from problems that should have been identified earlier in the analysis.

Sample Application

Assessment

Based on other aspects of Fred's performance, you determine that he is capable of writing higher quality reports on time. You also feel that he basically wants to succeed and is willing to improve his efforts.

Conclusion

Because of your assessment, you answer the P6 question "yes."

PERFORMANCE FACTOR	Yes	No
P6 Is the performer capable and willing to perform the task to expectations?	√	—
• Is the performer capable physically, mentally and emotionally of performing the task well?		
• Is the performer willing to perform to expectations?		

As before, a "yes" answer denotes that capability and willingness are probably not causing the gap. A "no" answer would have indicated that one or both of them are problematic-and that a change in either task/position or employment must be made.

P7: CAN PERSONAL ISSUES BE RULED OUT AS FACTORS INTERFERING WITH PERFORMANCE?

"Mental health can be hereditary. Your kids can drive you crazy."
WOODY ALLEN

The final question of the P-7 System asks: Could the performer have personal factors other than willingness—and which have not yet been addressed by the P-7 System—that are involved in the performance gap?

Typical of personal issues would be physical or mental health problems, family problems, financial problems, substance abuse and similar problems. Such issues can have significant impact on a performer's personal life and therefore interfere with job performance.

In looking at performance, personal issues are a touchy, sensitive—even possibly litigious—area. The reason is that, since they pertain to people's private lives, they involve information that people prefer to keep to themselves.

What the Answer Means

Note the way that the P7 question is structured. It's asked in such a way that "yes" and "no" answers remain consistent with how a factor is included or ruled out.

A "yes" means that personal issues are probably not a factor in the gap. A "no" means personal issues are probably involved to some extent in causing the gap. So, any P1 through P6 question answered "yes" is probably not implicated in performance. On the other hand, any question answered "no" is a highly probable cause—one that needs to be remedied.

Impact of Personal Issues

The personal issues that are the focus of P7 have an impact similar to—and possess the potential to be confused with—the capability and willingness factors of P6. This is natural, because P7 issues do impact performance in a fashion similar to capability and willingness—hopefully, however, more moderately and for a shorter time.

We even use similar language to describe P6 factors:

"Harry's health situation has incapacitated him somewhat." (Capability)

"Connie's depression over her family problems has really demotivated her and affected her performance." (Willingness)

If P7 issues become the rule rather than the exception, the issues present more of a P6 problem, and you need some help. A good strategy is to go directly to your HR department or Employee Assistance Program (EAP) representative.

Different geographic locations have different legal requirements and restrictions on dealing with personal issues in the workplace. The best and safest course is to link the performer up with HR professionals.

Still, the ball's not totally in your court. Performers have a shared responsibility with P7 issues. They still need to try contributing as much as possible, in spite of the situation. The manager's responsibility is to be empathetic, make temporary allowances and get the individual to HR or a company EAP or some similar course of action.

P7 Summary

Here's a quick-reference guide for your P7 response:

- Note that the question is worded so that, as with P1 through P6, a "no" answer flags a problem.
- By definition, personal issues are transitory, as opposed to chronic factors that diminish performance.
- It can be "touchy" to explore personal issues without invading a person's privacy; it's dangerous to attempt to deal with them without guidance and assistance from Human Resources.
- Managers have to walk a fine line between empathy and accommodation on one hand and tolerance of poor performance on the other. The job still needs to get done, and team morale will suffer, if others feel taken advantage of in this situation.

Sample Application

Assessment

You haven't identified any personal issues that could be affecting Fred's overall performance.

Conclusion

You therefore answer the P7 question "yes."

PERFORMANCE FACTOR	Yes	No
P7 Can personal issues be ruled out as factors interfering with performance? ▪ Does the performer have any physical or mental health Problems.? ▪ Is the performer experiencing any problems arising from issues such as family crises, financial trouble, substance abuse?	√	__

This ends the sample analysis of Fred. The next step is to interpret the answers to all of the P-7 System questions.

CHAPTER 9
SUMMARY OF P-7 ANALYSIS

Every performance problem that could be causing the gap in Fred's performance is addressed somewhere in the P-7 System. That fact is evident from the P-7 question chart on the next page and interpretation guidelines on the page adjacent to it.

The questions and answers not only identify the possible cause(s) of the gap, but also—and perhaps more importantly—the probable solution leading to better performance.

PERFORMANCE FACTOR	Yes	No
P1 Is this task designed for success? • Are others performing this task well? • Is it *realistic*, well *designed*? • Are adequate *resources* committed to it?	√	_
P2 Are expectations clear and matching? • Are expectations and standards certain to be fully understood? • Do expectations/priorities match?	_	√
P3 Has quality feedback been given: timely, constructive, balanced and honest? • Was feedback *positive* to motivate and reinforce expectations? • Was feedback *constructive* to get the person back on track and clarify expectations?	_	√
P4 Does the performer have the competence to perform the task to expectations? • Does the performer have the *skills?* • Does the performer have the *knowledge and experience?*	_	√
P5 Does the performer understand the importance of the task personally and to the organization? • Does the performer realize the gains/costs of good/poor performance (WIIFM and WNIIFM)? • Does the performer know the importance of the task to the organization and customers?	_	√
P6 Is the performer capable and willing to perform the task to expectations? • Is the performer capable physically, mentally and emotionally of performing the task well? • Is the performer willing to perform to expectations?	√	_
P7 Can personal issues be ruled out as factors interfering with performance? • Does the performer have any physical or mental health Problems? • Is the performer experiencing any problems arising from issues such as family crises, financial trouble, substance abuse?	√	_

PERFORMANCE-7 INTERPRETATION GUIDELINES

1. All questions must be answered as objectively as possible and must pertain specifically to the performer. No answer should be assumed, and there should be no easy "yes" answers.

2. "Yes" cannot be the answer to every question. If that were the case, there would be no performance gap! Everything necessary for performance would be present, and you would not be trying to solve a performance problem.

3. If the answers to P1 through P5 are "yes" and there is still a performance gap, you need to make a change:

    - If capability is the issue, change the performer's position.
    - If willingness is the issue, initiate steps to terminate the performer's employment.
    - If personal issues are interfering with performance, get the employee involved with HR.

    Those are the only three options left.

4. If any of the answers for P1 through P5 are "no," go back and reexamine them before going any further. It is difficult—if not impossible—to answer P6 because anything missing from the P1–P5 factors looks exactly like a problem in capability or willingness in how they impact performance.

PERFORMANCE IMPROVEMENT ACTION PLANNING

In the application example of Fred, we had several "no" answers. That means we have some work ahead to enable Fred to perform better.

Any question receiving a "no" answer calls for an action plan to reducing or eliminate the performance gap. At this point, your job is to outline one.

Response to P-7 "No" Answers

The chart on the next page is a quick reference guide on recommended responses to P-7 "no" answers.

P-7 FACTOR	ANSWER	RESPONSE
P1 – Task design	No	Improve task design: realism, design or resources.
P2 – Expectations	No	Clarify expectations; ensure they match.
P3 – Feedback	No	Increase timely, constructive, balanced feedback.
P4 – Competence	No	Provide appropriate coaching /training / development experiences.
P5 – Importance	No	Ensure personal and organizational understanding of importance.
P6 – Capability/ Willingness	No	*Capability:* Try to match another position to strengths. *Willingness:* Begin steps to change.
P7 – Personal issues	No	Get the person some help, usually from HR.

ACTION PLANNING FOR APPLICATION EXAMPLE

You need to have a discussion with Fred. Your first goal is to check and confirm your P-7 answers:

- What does Fred think you expect from him?
- What feedback have you given him on how well he is meeting your expectations?
- Is Fred comfortable writing the reports, or does he need some guidance or training?
- Have you confirmed for him why his reports are important and pointed out the personal gains and costs of his performance on reports?

You also need to confirm your "no" answers to Questions P2 through P5. If Fred agrees with your answers, you then need to: clarify expectations; provide feedback; give some guidance or coaching on report writing; explain the importance of his reports—in other words, take all the steps necessary to ensure that you can change every "no" answer to a "yes."

When you're done, Fred will have all of the factors in place to improve both the quality and timeliness of his reports. Performance will then start moving toward improvement and a decrease in the performance gap.

RESPONSIBILITY: MANAGER OR PERFORMER?

If you're a manager, after following the application example this far, you may be asking:

> *"Why shouldn't Fred be taking more initiative here? If he's missing some things he needs to perform better, he should speak up and go after them."*

Answer, Part 1

In most organizations, it's neither expected nor is it "okay" for Fred to take the initiative. An employee asking for any of the P-7 factors could be seen as whining, criticizing or complaining. Speaking out simply wouldn't be a safe strategy for a "Fred"—especially if he's a line-level or entry-level employee.

You have to make it safe for Fred. We would probably expect more senior or experienced employees to take more initiative in getting what they need to succeed, but few lower level employees will speak up unless they feel it's "safe."

Answer, Part 2

The basic responsibility of a manager is to produce results through others. If others don't know what we expect, don't have the right tools or training, or don't understand why their performance is important, then:

The buck always stops at the manager's desk.

By definition, managers are always, and ultimately, responsible for the performance of those who report to them in the organization.

ANALYSIS REQUIRES A PROFOUND CHANGE IN MANAGEMENT FOCUS

An important outcome of managers learning to use P-7 is that it begins to change their focus in identifying causes of performance problems. Managers initially focus primarily on the performer. The P-7 System broadens that focus to a much broader context, including themselves, as part of the problem.

Managers consequently revise how they frame and approach performance problems. P-7, in fact, literally becomes their performance management job description. Later chapters provide specific details of the focus change.

Until adopting the the P-7 System, most managers never realize that their actions-or inaction-can have such a powerful impact on performance. They, instead, tend to blame problems on the performer and think they can do very little to improve performance.

Managers come around to accepting what W. Edwards Deming said several decades ago:

> *"Most performance problems have little to do with the performer, but more to do with ineffective processes, procedures and management."*

Awareness of this fact comes from managers learning to analyze and improve performance with P-7. They typically take a big leap forward in leadership effectiveness and managerial maturity.

P-7 ANALYSIS ENABLES IMMEDIATE APPLICATION

Completed P-7 worksheets provide the framework for delineating and analyzing performance gaps. A completed worksheet, like the one on the next page for a direct report—in this case, for Fred in the sample analysis—becomes an invaluable performance improvement tool.

Blank worksheets for actual direct reports and for other aspects of P-7 are provided in the Appendix, along with worksheets expanding the P-7 System. Later pages expand the P-7 System to address performance issues with peers, teams, departments and, eventually, to an entire organization.

PERFORMANCE-7™ ANALYSIS WORKSHEET
DIRECT REPORT

GAP – Expected

> Fred completes assigned writing on time and with high quality, so that it does not require rewriting.

GAP – Actual

> Fred's writing assignments are late and so poorly written that I often have to rewrite them.

P-7 Analysis Questions

Answer each question as honestly as possible. Anything other than a completely firm "Yes" must be answered "No."

PERFORMANCE FACTOR	Yes	No
P1 Is the task designed for success? • Others performing this task well? • Task *realistic*, well *designed*? • Adequate *resources* committed?	√	
P2 Are expectations clear and matching? • Expectations & standards certain to be fully understood? • Expectations/priorities match?		√
P3 Has quality feedback been given: timely, constructive, balanced and honest? • Feedback *positive* to motivate & reinforce expectations? • Feedback *constructive* (gets back on track; clarifies expectations)?		√
P4 Does the performer have the competence to perform the task to expectations? • Performer has the *skills?* • Performer has the *knowledge* & *experience*?		√
P5 Does the performer understand the importance of the task personally and to the organization? • Performer realizes gains/costs of good/poor performance (WIIFM and WNIIFM)? • Performer knows importance of task to organization/customers?		√
P6 Is the performer capable and willing to perform the task to expectations? • Performer capable physically, mentally & emotionally of performing task well? • Performer willing to perform to expectations?	√	
P7 Can personal issues be ruled out as factors interfering with performance? • Performer experiencing any physical/mental health problems? • Performer having family/financial/substance abuse problems?	√	

CHAPTER 10

EXTENDING P-7 TO PEERS, MANAGERS, TEAMS & ORGANIZATIONS

THE PROBLEM

Overheard in the hallway:

"What's wrong Ellen? You seem upset."

"Yeah, I'm really frustrated. Steve's not holding up his end of this deal. He's late with deliverables. And when I do get them, they're so disorganized, they put me behind schedule because I have to dig out what I need!"

Peer issues like this are very common. Who hasn't been frustrated trying to get effective collaboration or support from peers or colleagues? As you read further in this chapter, you'll discover that we all play a bigger role in such problems than we might think.

THE PROCESS

Applying the P-7 process to situations beyond direct reports uses modified versions of the same questions asked in the last chapter. As with all applications of P-7, however, the process is consistent and the same, no matter the source or scale of the issue.

The core process is:

1. Define the problem in terms of a gap between expected and actual performance on the job.

2. Analyze the gap using the appropriate P-7 System questions.

3. Execute improvement actions, depending on your P-7 analysis.

PEER PERFORMANCE ISSUES

Although the P-7 factors remain the same as in a direct report analysis, the context is a bit more "touchy." Gaps involving peers are more sensitive simply because they are colleagues. You don't really have any power or authority over them. So you need to keep relationships collegial and realize coworkers may resent feedback that criticizes their efforts.

Working through an issue with your manager is even more sensitive than dealing with peers. You might try to push a direct report into performing better, but you would probably approach a similar problem with your manager very carefully, if at all.

One tendency remains constant no matter the situation, whether it's with a direct report, peer or manager. That's the strong inclination to pin substantial blame for a problem almost totally on someone else. Most people remain oblivious to their own role in a situation.

When we expect, but don't get, the support of another, it's all too easy to assume the role of victim. In some quarters, that may get some sympathy; but it certainly won't achieve better performance or business results.

APPLYING THE P-7 SYSTEM TO A PEER GAP

The P-7 process for dealing with peers applies to typical peer issues like the ones Ellen was dealing with:

> Steve isn't holding up his end of this deal. He delivers the goods late and with no organization, so Ellen is put behind and has extra work digging out the data she needs.

The process begins by defining the gap, then rewording each of the P-7 questions to apply the system to peer collaboration and support issues.

Defining the Gap

The first step is to state the problem in terms of the gap between expected (desired) performance and actual performance (see the sample P-7 Worksheet on page 70 for a good example).

> *Expected gap:* I expect Steve to be sharing the project data I need on time and in a well-organized fashion, so I can find the information I need quickly and keep our project on time.

> *Actual gap:* Steve is often late with the data, and the figures are so poorly organized that I have to waste time digging through the information to get what I need.

P-7 Questions for Peers

Note the framing of the following P-7 peer support questions below. Pay special attention to how much of the responsibility lies with you, the person needing the support. This reality is often an eye-opener when people understand that they need to consider their own involvement in an ongoing support problem.

P1 Question: Have I designed the task of collaborating so that it's easy for someone to support me?

In the peer situation of Ellen and Steve, Ellen needs to ask herself if she's asking Steve to crawl through broken glass, blindfolded to come to her assistance. It's not difficult to understand how Ellen and the rest of us typically pay more attention to our own tasks and how they are done, than we do to what others have to do to collaborate effectively.

In today's complex, far-flung, virtual organizations, people sometimes have limited understanding of the issues and challenges others have, trying to perform tasks to support them. Even if Steve works just down the hall from Ellen, she may, because of differences in technical specialties or function, have little understanding of what Steve actually has to do to support her.

The P1 question covers more than "what they have to do" to support you. It also gets to the heart of how the collaborative relationship is structured and how the process of support is designed. You have to ask yourself: Am I optimizing the entire collaborative process from the peer's perspective, making it easy for them to do business with me?

As with the direct report P-7 questions, you have to assume the answer is "no" unless you're absolutely certain that, from their perspective, it would be a "yes." In other words, when you're in P-7 territory, you're always guilty until proven innocent.

Exploring P1 issues

Ellen can explore P1 further by asking Steve questions such as:

- How realistic/easy is it for you to give me the support/ collaboration I need?
- What actually has to occur, on your end, to give me the collaboration I need?

- What barriers get in the way of making it easier to provide this support to me?
- How would you suggest redesigning our collaboration to make it work better for both of us?
- Do you have the resources to give us what is required?

Answer to the P1 Question

Ellen notes that other colleagues having similar sharing tasks seem to get her the data on time—and that it's better organized. She consequently doesn't feel that the task is a problem at this point. Ellen should therefore answer P1 "yes," but with the intent to further explore the issues with Steve by asking the questions above.

As with a direct report issue, P-7 task design again involves looking at realism, design and resources. There's no "silver-bullet" guarantee that this will result in an improved collaboration process. At the very least, however, you'll have a better understanding of, and perhaps appreciation for, what Steve is facing—and, ultimately, a better collaborative relationship.

The improved relationship Ellen experiences will have begun because she cared enough to investigate how she could work better with Steve, rather than simply blaming him for the gap in performance. Blaming him not only wouldn't fix the gap, but it could also poison Ellen's future working relationship with Steve.

P2 Question: Does the person know exactly what I expect/require of them?

Expectations continue to be the area where foul-ups are most common —and where the dreaded "should" again plays its sinister role. Just as was the case with direct reports, it's all too easy for Ellen to assume that Steve "should" know what she wants.

Exploring P2 issues

Exploration of issues with peers is also similar to that involving direct reports. However, the simple, "Do you know what I need/expect/require?" won't work. The reason: Steve will probably answer, "yes." As before, he may be convinced that he actually does understand what Ellen needs.

Ellen therefore needs to compare "pictures" of expectations so that both Steve and she are on the same page in understanding what's required. She simply has to ask Steve what he thinks she needs from him; listen carefully; then work to align the two pictures of expectations so they match.

When approached effectively, seldom will a conversation of this nature have anything but a favorable outcome. The typical results are improved collaboration and working relationships between both parties.

Answer to the P2 Question

Although Steve probably understands Ellen's time lines in the sample case, Ellen hasn't been as clear as she should have been in defining how she wants the information formatted.

Steve therefore doesn't know precisely what Ellen requires of him. So Ellen has to answer the P2 question with a "no."

P3 Question—Have I given the performer feedback about the nature of the gap?

As noted earlier, feedback to direct reports is sometimes inadequate. That pales in comparison with feedback to peers which is often completely absent. The reason is the natural reluctance to bring up a problem, start an argument or create a conflict situation with a colleague face to face.

That reluctance typically disappears, however, out of the colleague's earshot. How often have you heard someone complaining around the water cooler about how an unhelpful peer or coworker is victimizing them. The presumed offender is usually the last to know there's a problem.

Importance of First-person Statements in Giving Feedback

Dealing with workplace conflict and conflict management are beyond the scope of this work. Numerous excellent books and articles have been written on those subjects.

This is the place, however, to share a useful technique for bringing up collaboration issues. The tip is to use first-person *(I, we)* statements, as opposed to second-person *(you–you–you)* statements.

A typical second-person statement would be:

Steve, you're being uncooperative. Your figures are late and buried in disorganized reports that make it really hard for me to get my lab work done on time. You don't seem to care how hard you make my job. I'm falling behind on this project . . . because of you.

Such an upset, blaming tone (you...you...you) is certain to put Steve on the defensive. Rather than getting his cooperation, this approach will invariably lead to more anger, defensiveness and alienation. If Ellen confronts Steve like this, she's likely to minimize his willingness to collaborate on the project.

Ellen is much more likely to get Steve's cooperation if she uses a first-person statement, framed like this:

*"I have a problem/concern/etc., when (**the gap or problem occurs**), because (**consequences of the situation**) . . . so, I need your help."*

Wording of such a first-person statement could read something like this:

Steve, I have a problem when the data summaries are late—also when the most important data is buried with less significant stuff. It takes extra time both to recover from the lateness and to keep the project on schedule when I have to search for the key numbers. Can we talk about how to keep this from happening?

This statement contains the four key features of an effective first-person statement:

- States the problem objectively, without blaming the other person.
- Makes a statement of fact, observing that a problem exists, rather than sounding like the person speaking is judge and jury.
- Cites consequences rather than focusing on selfish needs—at the same time sheds light on the importance of collaboration (think P5 . . . understanding importance). The consequences become the primary problem, not a person's behavior.
- Requests help instead of trying to fix the blame.

First-person statements have proven to be much more effective than second-person statements in dealing with performance issues. That's true across the board—with direct reports, peers, managers, or a team member.

In framing first-person statements for peer collaboration:

- Avoid blaming and shaming. Even though it may be deserved, it gets you nothing but defensiveness and makes future collaboration more difficult.

- State the problem as fairly and objectively as possible. Try to look at the issue from the peer's perspective.

- Focus on the resulting negative consequences to build understanding of importance (P5)—and so that the peer doesn't perceive the issue as being all about what *you* need."

- Don't try to "balance" feedback as you might do in a performance review. Statements like, *"I really appreciate most of what you do to support me, BUT…"* are easily seen as disingenuous.

Answer to the P3 Question

Ellen hasn't given Steve clear feedback on the problem she's having with disorganized data. She's only griped about his being late.

Steve hasn't received full feedback on the nature of the gap. So, Ellen has no choice but to answer the P3 question "no."

P4 Question: Does the person know HOW to provide the collaboration or support I need?

Competency isn't typically a primary cause of peer support issues. Still, it's advisable to take a brief look at it during analysis.

That's particularly true when the support you need consists of specialized knowledge, training or significant experience on the job—also when considering whether you need to do a better job of sharing information or communicating in order to get the support you need.

Remedying Missing Competency

A peer without the requisite knowledge, training or experience may have your best interests in mind, but simply may not possess the competence to deliver what you need. In such cases, you may need to assist in developing or accelerating the person's competency—that, or identify a more promising source of support.

If it's necessary to approach the issue of competency, it's best do do it with sensitivity because of the nature of peer relationships. Few people will respond well to:

"No offense Harry, but you don't know what you're doing."
OR
"That's OK Tom, I'll find someone else who's more capable to help me."

Plan any coaching, mentoring or advisory attempts to help improve a colleague's support very judiciously to ensure you don't risk damaging trust and collegial relations.

Mark Twain summed up that danger with the sage observation:

"Nothing scares me so much as someone coming to do me a favor."

You'll get the best results through collaboration. Don't try to "fix" a peer or "make the colleague a better person."

Answer to the P4 Question

Ellen has sized up Steve as an experienced, professional colleague who definitely knows how to put a report together and how to stick to a time line. He therefore certainly knows how to supply the support she needs.

Ellen's answer to the P4 question is consequently inevitable. It has to be "yes."

P5 Question: Does the peer understand the importance to them (personal gain/loss), and to the organization, of meeting the expectations?

P-7 System research shows that the P5 factor joins P2 (expectations) and P3 (feedback) as the factors most often impaired in peer support gaps. There's a lot of collaborative ground covered by the issues in under-standing task importance. Recall that this is also the motivational/inspirational factor in gaining others' committed performance.

Understanding Personal Importance

The two additional questions shown on the next page must be asked to better understand the full significance of personal importance.

Additional questions:

1. *Is there a gain (to them) for providing support (WIIFM)?*

   This doesn't mean a bribe or a kickback or monetary remuneration. Answering this question requires seeing through the other person's lenses and examining: *"What's in it for me to provide this for you?"*

   This is of particular importance when providing effective support that requires the other person to go outside the normal scope of their defined job. Fortunately, the missing ingredient is usually fairly simple to supply. A little appreciation and recognition of others' efforts goes a long way to supplying WIIFM.

   As is typically the case with appreciation and recognition, our hearts are more pure than our habits. In the rush of daily and weekly activity, your golden intentions get lost in the shuffle. Most of the peers who support your activities aren't expecting adoration or lavish praise.

   Simply noticing, acknowledging and appreciating a person from time to time goes a long way. To quote Mark Twain once again: *"A good compliment will last me about a month."*

2. *Is there any cost (to the peer) for their lack of support?*

   Typically, when others don't support us well, there are few costs for their actions or inaction on our behalf. Except for nagging, begging or pleading, we don't really have authority to do much when support performance is inadequate.

   One solution could be going to the powers that be (their manager, for example) and asking for assistance to improve the support you get. This strategy, however, is often of limited effectiveness for a couple of reasons:

   - The fact that you are being shorted and there are no sanctions for ineffective support or collaboration may be signaling that their boss has other priorities and that your needed support may not be high on the priority list.

   - Any sanctions leveled as the result of intervention by a colleague's manager will almost ensure that the support, if it improves at all, will be delivered through gritted teeth—and that your future relationship with this peer could be tense.

For these reasons, along with the fact that positive reinforcement is much more powerful, the best strategy is to use a carrot, rather than a stick, to improve collaborative support. Heed the folk wisdom that says: *"You attract a lot more flies with honey than with vinegar."*

Understanding Importance to the Organization

Research leading to the P-7 System, and experience implementing the system, show that recognizing organizational importance is a potentially powerful, but much underutilized, factor in increasing collaborative support. It's not so much that the need for support has to have earth-shaking implications; it's that people simply need to understand why their support is important.

They also need to know how their support will be used and what happens when it's missing. The focus is on the power of knowing "why."

Generally, business communication is better at explaining what is important and not so good at explaining why. We're all quite good at telling others what they should be doing, especially since we've been honing that skill since we were all in the sandbox. Building others' understanding of why is what fosters the understanding that yields motivation, commitment and inspiration.

The following scenario illustrates the importance of the "why" in business communication. It's a situation in which you may very well have found yourself on both sides of the table.

You need Matt's summary of the prior week's sales activities by 8:30 on Monday mornings. Matt is habitually late, usually getting the data to your office around noon.

Matt reasons that since you go into a business planning session every Monday morning—and it seldom ends much before noon—you won't have time to read or use the reports anyway until the afternoon.

He also knows that your morning meeting doesn't pertain to sales activities, so he may feel that your insistence on having reports by 8:30 is a "way to throw your weight around and show your colleagues how important you are."

What he doesn't know is that you have privately committed to sharing that summary of the sales reports with your counterpart in the Zurich office (eight hours ahead) by close of business every

Monday. Every time you miss that deadline, you're embarrassed and have to make apologies for the "lack of consistency here at the home office."

The crux of the problem, therefore, is that Matt neither knows why you need his data, nor what actually happens when it's late. As a result, he assumes that your need is trivial and puts your request low on his priority list.

How often do situations like this one occur every working day? How often has something like this happened to you?

P5 Factor Key Points

The fifth factor of the P-7 System ensures that others have personal gains—appreciation or reciprocity for collaborating effectively. This significantly increases the odds of getting good support. It also ensures that the person understands WHY you need their help, how important it is, and what happens when it's not forthcoming. That understanding builds their ongoing commitment to giving you what you need.

Failure to properly communicate with, and recognize the efforts of, those who support you can cost you dearly in terms of ongoing collaboration and support. Once again, a barrier to providing understanding is *"should"*—*"They **should** know why I need it."*

Even worse is: *"I don't think I have to explain; he **should** be doing what I ask of him."* More explanations of *"WHY"* and *"Thanks for your help"* go a long way in sustaining better collaboration.

Answer to the P5 question

Ellen has not given Steve any direct gain for supporting her, other than not hearing her gripe. There are, however, consequences for lack of support: It's going to reflect poorly on both Ellen and Steve if Ellen keeps missing her deadline.

The bigger issue is that Steve probably doesn't understand the consequences of his delays. Ellen definitely has to answer the P5 question with a "no."

P6 & P7: Questions: Is the person capable and willing to provide the necessary collaboration; can personal issues be ruled out?

Progress Check

The progress the P-7 System has delivered so far in the sample case is summarized in the first five answers on the page 70 sample worksheet: P1-yes, P2-no, P3-no, P4-yes and P5-no. That review paves the way toward completing the worksheet.

Going Forward

In addressing issues of whether someone is capable and willing to collaborate (P6 factor) or whether external/personal issues are involved (P7 factor), you have less latitude than in dealing with a direct report issue. For example, when the issue is one of your direct reports being in the wrong position and not being willing to perform or having interfering external issues, you can play a more involved role than when you're dealing with a peer or colleague issue.

Lack of authority and sensitive personal issues coming into play are factors that make options in dealing with P7 issues far more limited than with the first five factors. You've already seen how appealing to a higher authority may get some short-term results but do little to foster a better collaborative working relationship.

The good news is that the majority of your collaboration/support issues can be addressed by using the powerful leverage you have gained with factors P1 through P5. Ensuring that you have provided the P1 through P5 factors will go a long way toward getting you the support you need.

Take Some Ownership

To return to a theme, the responsibility for improved collaboration is primarily yours. In the sample case, Ellen is the one who needs improved collaboration. Once you begin to better understand how the P-7 factors affect collaboration, it will becomes more obvious that you are responsible for setting the stage to optimize collaboration.

P7 Peer Questions

Framing the P-7 factors to ensure that you get the support you need leads to understanding that, as with direct report issues, you have to take the initiative in getting the support you need.

Ask yourself the following peer questions before blaming your peer for collaboration problems:

PEER QUESTIONS

TASK	Have I designed the collaborative process to make it easy or hard for others to support me effectively?
EXPECTATIONS	Have I ensured that my expectations are clear and understood by those whose support I need?
FEEDBACK	Have I given timely, constructive feedback so others know whether or not they are supporting me well?
COMPETENCY	Have I done everything possible to ensure that others have the specialized knowledge, information or skills to support me competently?
UNDERSTANDING	Have I ensured that others see a gain for their support and understand the costs, to them, to me and to the organization of not supporting me well? Have I ensured that they know WHY their support is important, not just to me, but also the organization?

Your Responsibility

The phrasing of the peer questions make it clear that much of the responsibility for setting the stage and enabling others to support you well begins with you. This stage of analysis is therefore similar to applying the P-7 factors to a direct report performance gap.

If you pause for a moment to think about it, this ownership is actually good news for you. If the first five factors of P-7 have that kind of impact on the level of performance or support you're going to receive from others, it's to your advantage to have as much control over them as possible.

You've already discovered the bad news aspect of the first five P-7 System factors: If they're missing, they're the primary causes of most of your performance problems with others.

So you're both enabled and accountable to use the P-7 factors to maximize others' ability to deliver the performance necessary to produce results. In the final analysis, this is what performance leadership with a direct report or a colleague is all about.

Peer Analysis Summary

Key points to keep in mind when applying the P-7 System to a peer are:

- Through your actions, you can maximize or minimize the probability that someone else can perform or support you well.
- The word "should" is again a barrier: "He should understand what I need" or "She should be supportive, regardless of the circumstances."
- The causes of most collaboration and support issues are found in factors P1 through P5. That's good news because factors P6 and P7 can be difficult to assess and handle with a peer.
- The real key to getting peer commitment is to see through the peer's eyes and consider: What's in it for them (WIIFT).

Application

A sample P-7 Worksheet for the example peer support issue appears on the next page. A blank P-7 Worksheet for peer issues is provided in the Appendix. Use this worksheet to identify a current peer performance gap; then apply the P-7 System to analyze and improve the support you require from others.

PERFORMANCE-7™ ANALYSIS WORKSHEET

PEER/COLLEAGUE

GAP – Expected

> Steve delivers his data on time
> and so well organized that I have
> what I need to stay on schedule.

GAP – Actual

> Steve delivers his data so late
> and so disorganized that I have
> to work overtime figuring it out.

P-7 Analysis Questions

*Answer each question as honestly as possible. Anything
other than a completely firm "Yes" must be answered "No."*

PERFORMANCE FACTOR	Yes	No
P1 Is this collaboration task designed for success? Is collaboration structured well so it's easier for the peer to give me what I need?	√	
P2 Are expectations clear and matching? ▪ Peer fully understand my expectations? ▪ Expectations/priorities match?		√
P3 Have I given timely, quality feedback? ▪ *Positive* feedback to motivate & reinforce expectations? ▪ *Constructive* feedback to get back on track; clarify expectations?		√
P4 Is the peer competent to supply what I need? ▪ Has the *skills?* ▪ Has the *knowledge & experience?*	√	
P5 Does the colleague understand the importance of the task personally and to the organization? ▪ Realizes gains/costs of good/poor performance (WIIFM and WNIIFM)? ▪ Knows importance of task to me and the organization?		√
P6 Is the peer capable and willing to perform the task to expectations? ▪ Physically, mentally & emotionally able to perform the task well? ▪ Willing to give me what I need?	√	
P7 Can personal issues be ruled out as factors interfering with performance? ▪ Transitory problems? ▪ Transitory organizational problems?	√	

P-7 AND TEAM PERFORMANCE ISSUES

A team issue is defined as a performance problem that is fairly consistent across the entire team. Let's look at a team performance gap with a sales manager in the organization:

Scenario: A sales manager is upset.

"I've repeatedly stressed the importance of generating more customer referrals, but my team doesn't do it. I don't know if they're unwilling to put forth the effort, or if they don't see the payoff."

Assume that you're that upset sales manager who doesn't understand why the team doesn't generate referrals. In applying the P-7 factors to a problem in team performance, once again, it's how you articulate each question that changes its application.

The basic system and logic always remain constant. You can tailor your P-7 questions exactly to the "referral generation gap" you are analyzing. Again, as you work your way through the factors that are hopefully now becoming familiar to you, consider a real performance issue you may have with a team that you would like to address.

Here are the P-7 questions applied to our team example:

P-7 QUESTIONS: TEAM

Factor	Question
P1	Have we designed the process and procedures of generating referrals to make it easier or harder for salespeople to do them effectively?
P2	Have we stated a clear expectation that generating more referrals is a high priority for our sales group?
P3	Have we given our salespeople timely, constructive feedback on referral generation?
P4	Do salespeople have the requisite skills and know the best techniques for generating more sales referrals?
P5	Do salespeople see WIIFM for generating more referrals? Are there any consequences for lack of referral generation? Do they realize why, in the big picture, referrals are so valuable to the organization and to them? Is there any downside for them in trying to generate referrals?

P-7 QUESTIONS: TEAM

Factor	Question
P6	Are the salespeople capable and willing to do what is necessary to generate more referrals?
P7	Can we rule out any outside factors that may be impeding their ability to generate more referrals?

Analysis

As before, an unequivocal "yes" means that this is probably not the cause of our referral deficit, while a "no" answer means that we have some work to do with that P-7 factor.

Action

For illustration, let's say that you answered questions P4 and P5 as "no." That pattern of answers (found on the example P-7 Team Worksheet on page 73) indicates the following action plan to close the referral gap:

1. For P4: Utilize coaching, training-and-development activities and exercises to strengthen the skill base of the sales team in effective methods of generating sales referrals.

2. For P5: Ensure that every salesperson on the team knows WIIFM (the payback and incentive for them personally) for referral generation, the consequences of not generating adequate referrals and, most importantly, why producing a steady flow of sales referrals is critical for sales productivity and organizational success.

Means of accomplishment include coaching, sales meetings, or presentations and testimonials/demonstrations from salespeople with high referral rates. As noted previously, for either direct report or peer performance problems, a "yes" answer rules out a factor, while a "no" answer directs your performance improvement action plans.

The completed P-7 Worksheet for this example is found on the next page. A blank Team P-7 Worksheet is also found in the Appendix. Apply the worksheet activity to a team issue and see how your analysis helps you improve performance.

PERFORMANCE-7™ ANALYSIS WORKSHEET

TEAM ISSUE

GAP – Expected

> The sales team should generate at least 3 new referrals per month, per salesperson to meet our sales goals.

GAP – Actual

> The sales team averages less than one new referral per month/person making it hard to meet sales goals.

P-7 Analysis Questions

Answer each question as honestly as possible. Anything other than a completely firm "Yes" must be answered "No."

PERFORMANCE FACTOR	Yes	No
P1 Is this team task designed for success? Is it realistic and well structured? Are adequate resources committed to it?	√	__
P2 Are expectations clear and matching? ▪ Team fully understands my expectations? ▪ Expectations/priorities match?	√	__
P3 Has timely, quality feedback been given to the entire team? ▪ *Positive* feedback to motivate & reinforce expectations? ▪ *Constructive* feedback to get back on track, clarify expectations?	√	__
P4 Is the team competent to perform the task? ▪ Has the *skills?* ▪ Has the *knowledge & experience?*	__	√
P5 Do team members fully understand the importance of the task both personally and to the organization? ▪ Realize gains/costs of good/poor performance (WIIFM and WNIIFM)? ▪ Knows importance of the task to the organization?	__	√
P6 Is the team capable and willing to perform the task to expectations? ▪ Physically, mentally & emotionally able to perform the task well? ▪ Willing to perform to expectations?	√	__
P7 Can personal issues be ruled out as factors interfering with performance? ▪ Transitory problems? ▪ Transitory organizational problems?	√	__

Next, we'll explore how scalable the P-7 analysis system is and if it can be applied to larger teams, a department, a division or even an entire organization.

ORGANIZATIONAL PERFORMANCE ISSUES

When addressing performance on larger scales, P-7 scales-up right along with you, analyzing causes of gaps at the higher level. As you've already seen, the wording may change, but the system and factors are basically the same.

We can illustrate P-7 scalability using a real-life example of a disguised entire organization suffering from poor customer service. We'll call the organization High Tech, Inc. As before, consider application to a similar broad issue for your organization as you work through this actual real-world example.

Customer Service Gap

The senior management team of High Tech called our consultant team "to develop customer service training" for their employees. Their marketing department had recently surveyed the customer base for the very first time and found that customers were unhappy with their service.

Even though the top managers had already prescribed training to improve customer service, we took them through an organizational level P-7 analysis.

At a minimum, we told them, P-7 will help us organize our inquiry into the gap. More importantly, however, we continued, P-7 may be able to rule out some organizational factors and identify others. That could direct our recommendations for improvement initiatives.

As in other applications, we tailored our P-7 questions to the appropriate scope of the issue at hand. The following subsections describe the questions facing High Tech, Inc.

P1 Question: Is the task of delivering quality customer service designed for success at High Tech?

Situation at High Tech

As usual, we looked at task design as: realism, task design and resources. Almost immediately, the wheels started to wobble. High Tech had cut costs to the bone, ensuring that customer-handling expectations for High Tech personnel were highly unrealistic.

Complicating the issue was the fact that although customer contact volume had increased considerably with the introduction of new, more complex products, the organization was still using customer interface processes and procedures (task design) that were now outmoded and perilously shaky.

To top it all off, High Tech's cost-cutting measures included outsourcing small customer service requests to outside call centers. Some customers were complaining loudly about: "*. . . having to talk to someone in Bangalore about a service issue in Boise.*"

Attempting to deliver customer service "on the cheap" left High Tech with far too few resources to handle customer requests and concerns. Resources they devoted to service may have sufficed a year back; but for existing expectations, they were totally inadequate.

Answer to the High Tech P1 Question

Since task design and resources were impaired— not to mention realism—there was only one possible answer to the P1 question: a resounding "no."

P2 Question: Are expectations clear and matching?

Situation at High Tech

Although personnel in customer interface and service areas were aware of the company's service expectations, they saw them as unrealistic and unachievable; they therefore largely disregarded them. What's more, personnel outside of the defined customer-interface areas didn't even see service as an expectation of their job. When they encountered a customer issue, they routinely either ignored it or passed it on to another area, because they considered the issue ". . . not my job."

In addition, there were incentives for not taking action. Ignoring a request for service had no traceable consequences. On the other hand, attempting to service a client with inadequate means could result in a negative report. (Think about how negative consequences for trying to help would impact Factor P5.)

Answer to the High Tech P2 Question

High Tech staff therefore soon learned that when it came to customer complaints, "Ignorance was bliss." The answer to the P2 question was also definitely, "no."

P3 Question: Has timely, constructive feedback been given?

Situation at High Tech

The only High Tech staff who received any feedback were those in defined customer-interface and customer-support areas. No organizational system was present for measuring and monitoring current service levels other than their recent first-time survey. Therefore, the rest of High Tech's employees didn't know that service wasn't up to par.

Furthermore, since they really didn't consider customer service to be part of their job, they regarded the customer complaints they did hear as "the usual griping and moaning."

Answer to the High Tech P3 Question

No feedback left only one answer to the High Tech P3 question: still another "no."

P4 Question: Are the skills and knowledge for customer service in place?

Situation at High Tech

High Tech had done very limited customer service training over the past few years. All of the staff in defined service areas received some training, but most employees had little understanding of what constituted good service.

Answer to the High Tech P4 Question

The answer to the High Tech P4 question was predictable: Again, "no."

P5 Question: Do High Tech staff understand the personal and organizational importance of delivering good customer service.

Precious little personal understanding and few incentives for effective customer service existed anywhere in High Tech. Even in their call center, reps received incentives only for handling customer calls in a minimum of time—nothing for high-quality service. Reps consequently tended to hurry customers to end their call.

Outside of defined customer areas, staff members saw neither personal consequences for poor service nor any gain for good service. The reason, as cited in the P2 discussion above, was that they didn't view customer service as an expected part of their job. Furthermore, they had experienced negative consequences (let no good deed go unpunished) for trying to help (taking too long on a call with a customer).

Although staff realized that customer service was important organizationally, they were also concerned that spending a lot of money in that area might detract from available resources for their own areas—not to mention constraining funds available for their compensation. P5 was certainly a "no."

P6 Question: Are High Tech people capable and willing to deliver good customer service?

High Tech's staff was largely both capable and willing to deliver better service. Although High Tech hadn't specifically hired against a "service mentality" profile, they did have an employee base that was capable of, and wanted to, deliver better service. The answer to the P6 question was consequently a "yes."

P-7 Question: Can personal issues be ruled out as a cause of the gap?

When scaling the P-7 System to the organizational level, this question, because of its personal focus, obviously isn't as relevant as the others. Evidence of some "organizational malaise" or cultural or morale issue could have been explored; but answers to the six previous questions provided ample information to work with.

Conclusion

With answers to the P1, P2, P3, P4 and P5 questions all being "no," it was virtually inevitable that service would suffer. P-7 analysis made it abundantly clear that High Tech needed more than the "training" issue that they had identified on their own.

P-7 ACTION PLAN FOR HIGH TECH

The P-7 Worksheet for High Tech's organizational issues on page 80 provided the framework for planning. As in other applications of the P-7 System,, "no" answers drive the action plans.

Plan Specifics

For High Tech, the P-7 action plan was to:

P1: a) Update and redesign processes and procedures to allow for effective service delivery; b) provide additional resources needed to make service delivery a realistic, viable certainty.

P2: a) Make expectations realistic and manageable for service personnel; b) for everyone else, integrate the importance of fulfilling customer needs into every single High Tech job description, across all areas of the organization—make it clear that everyone at High Tech has to be in customer service.

P3: Share customer service data and customer complaints/feedback across the organization so that everyone can see where problems exist and also so that people can take pride as performance increases.

P4: a) Initiate customer service training; it's necessary, but not sufficient to turn the problem around; b) focus on both leadership and culture change efforts.

P5: a) Make everyone aware of how customer service pays off for them, how it costs them when it's not good and how their current role contributes to effective customer service; b) reinforce this message with repeated coaching and explaining, up and down the management ranks.

P6: No action required. The workforce appeared to be pretty capable and willing to improve service, so capability and willingness were probably not a cause of the customer service issue. Recall that the P6 question received a "yes" response because of the preceding "no" answers.

P7: No action required. As noted above, personal issues were not really applicable at this scale. The closest resemblance was an overall organizational culture interfering with performance.

Note how much of High Tech's problem came from:

- P1 – outmoded and under-resourced tasks/processes
- P2 – expectations running the gamut from unrealistic to nonexistent
- P3 – little or no service feedback
- P4 – lack of appropriate training
- P5 – lack of awareness and understanding of the importance and impact of service.

The sample P-7 Organizational Worksheet appears on the next page. Blank organizational worksheets are provided in the Appendix.

PERFORMANCE-7™ ANALYSIS WORKSHEET

ORGANIZATIONAL ISSUE

GAP – Expected

Staff should deliver excellent customer service to stay competitive and succeed in the marketplace.

GAP – Actual

Customer feedback indicates that High Tech's customer service is poor and ignores customer concerns.

P-7 Analysis Questions

Answer each question as honestly as possible. Anything other than a completely firm "Yes" must be answered "No."

PERFORMANCE FACTOR	Yes	No
P1 Is this organozational task designed for success? Is it realistic and well structured? Are adequate resources committed to it?		√
P2 Are expectations clear and matching across the organization? ▪ Staff fully understands expectations? ▪ Expectations/priorities match?		√
P3 Has timely, quality feedback been given across the organization? ▪ *Positive* feedback to motivate & reinforce expectations? ▪ *Constructive* feedback to get back on track, clarify expectations?		√
P4 Are individuals competent to perform the task? ▪ Possess the *skills?* ▪ Possess the *knowledge & experience?*		√
P5 Does staff fully understand the importance of the task both personally and to the organization? ▪ Realize gains/costs of good/poor performance (WIIFM and WNIIFM)? ▪ Understand importance of task to the organization?		√
P6 Is staff capable and willing to perform the task to expectations? ▪ Physically, mentally & emotionally able to perform the task well? ▪ Willing to perform to expectations?	√	
P7 Can outside issues be ruled out as factors interfering with performance? ▪ Transitory personal problems? ▪ Transitory organizational problems?	√	

Summary

There's no rocket science or counter-intuitive discovery occurring in the P-7 analysis and plan for High Tech. What P-7 does accomplish when applied to an organization is to ensure that we look at all of the factors . . . that we don't rush to conclusions concerning cause . . . and that we put resources into the right solutions to best close the gaps.

Without this type of analysis, employees, managers and organizations have been known to throw a lot of time, money and resources at fixing the wrong problem—then wondering why the gap is still present.

USING P-7 AS AN ORGANIZATIONAL CONSULTANT

As the applications in this chapter have shown, P-7 is scalable to any level; and the concepts are broad enough to cover problems with colleagues, teams, departments, organizations and virtually any entity that may have a performance gap. Once you become comfortable with P-7's application, you'll find yourself viewing most organizational performance issues through a P-7 lens.

The Power of P-7

Every day, across every organization, managers are wrestling with gaps and shortfalls in performance. The P-7 System gives you a universal template to be applied any time something should be happening . . . but isn't.

By ensuring that P-7 elements are in place early on, you can optimize your chances at successful execution. Using P-7 on the front-end won't ensure that a poorly conceived plan will succeed, but it will ensure that a well-crafted plan has every opportunity for success.

P-7's Broad Application

Hopefully, you now realize that P-7—because it's based on those fundamental principles that enable performance in any context—can be universally applied to any performance gap, anywhere in the organization. Once you master its use, P-7 becomes your all-purpose performance tool.

Immediate Application

This chapter has given you several options for application. You can choose a performance issue involving:

- A team
- A department or division
- An entire organization

Whatever the application, however, the process remains constant:

1. Clearly delineate the gap.
2. Apply the appropriate P-7 questions by using the applicable P-7 Worksheet provided in the Appendix.
3. Take appropriate improvement actions, based on your P-7 answers.

CHAPTER 11

APPLICATIONS OF PERFORMANCE-7™
FOR INDIVIDUAL CONTRIBUTORS: THE P-7 CONTRACT

You now understand the P-7 System and how to apply it to performance issues with direct reports, peers, teams and an entire organization. Next, you'll see how the system also can guide performance while building self-leadership for individual contributors in your organization.

This application had its origin a few years ago when we were asked to teach the P-7 System to non-management employees, a group of engineers in a defense plant. The goal was to increase their sense of self-leadership and performance on the job. As we progressed through this challenge, it became obvious that it was a natural fit to extend P-7 to this situation.

An unforeseen issue in scheduling the training resulted in the training group learning about the P-7 System before their managers became familiar with it. Almost immediately, the engineers began using the P-7 factors to challenge practices that they felt were impairing their ability to perform at their best.

The unprepared managers were suddenly besieged by impatient employees making demands like:

"This project's not designed for success...we're being set up to fail!"

"We need clear expectations, so we don't work on this for weeks and find out that it's not what you wanted . . . like last time."

The lesson learned is that managers need to learn P-7 first—before their employees start using it.

THE PERFORMANCE-7™ CONTRACT

From what you've read so far, you can see that teaching P-7 to employees can be a bit risky. The reason: Once you let the P-7 genie out of the bottle, there's no way to get it back in. P-7 for employees truly spells out a fundamental, implicit contract between employees and the organization.

This contract sets two clear expectations:

1. As an organization, we have a right to your best performance and contribution on the job.

2. As an employee, you have a right to leadership and support (the P-7 factors) that allow you to do your best.

In other words, there's a P-7 "contract" between an organization and its employees, governing employee rights and responsibilities.

P-7 CONTRACT FOR EMPLOYEES

EVERY EMPLOYEE HAS THE RIGHT TO:

1. Be assigned tasks that are designed for success (realistic, designed right, adequately resourced).

2. Ask for, and receive, a clear, accurate up-front understanding of task expectations—no surprises, assumptions or *"shoulds."*

3. Receive timely, quality feedback that keeps them on track and recognizes good performance.

4. The training and development necessary to equip them to do the job competently.

5. Clear understanding of the gain for good performance, the costs of poor performance, plus why the task is important to the organization and its customers.

6. Be assigned to tasks that fit their capabilities and strengths.

7. Help from HR when personal factors interfere with their ability to perform to their best.

EVERY EMPLOYEE, IN RETURN, HAS THE RESPONSIBILITY TO:

1. Give the company their best efforts and perform effectively (P6—willingness).

2. Keep trying to perform effectively even when faced with outside, personal issues (P7—personal issues).

PEOPLE CARE ABOUT THEIR JOBS

No matter whether you agree or disagree philosophically with the statements of P-7 rights. . . . whether or not they're applicable in your current organizational culture . . . this much is certain, based on our experience instilling line employees with an understanding of what they need to perform, via P-7:

- Most people honestly want to do their best on the job (Theory Y lives!). An insignificant minority may come to work without caring; but most employees want to leave the workplace feeling: *"I've done my job well...I've had an impact...I've made a difference."*

- Setting high expectations and holding people accountable for achieving them sends powerful messages of trust, confidence and personal regard. All of these are critical to high commitment and engagement.

- Letting employees know that they have a right to things such as well-designed tasks, clear expectations and necessary training—plus, that it's OK to ask for them if they are missing— is very empowering and motivating.

Earlier we discussed reasons why employees don't speak up more or take more initiative when P-7 attributes are missing on the job. If people understand that they have a right to these factors and can safely ask for them, their proactive involvement changes dramatically.

Much of the action that occurs in such an environment centers around P1 through P5. *"All hell breaks loose"* (a quote from one senior manager) in situations where:

- Employees learn that they have the right to challenge situations in which they have been set up to fail (P1).

- Expectations are vague or ambiguous (P2) and where feedback is sparse or non-existent (P3).

- Training has been inadequate (P4) or understanding/ motivation (P5) is lacking.

Fortunately, these are also usually easily addressed issues.

Next, we'll extend P-7 concepts to projects or initiatives that involve either individual contributors or employee teams.

CHAPTER 12

P-7 APPLIED TO PROJECTS

Define a project as a series of tasks to be executed in a coordinated fashion, and the P-7 System also becomes applicable to projects. In project application, you can use P-7 three ways:

- Prospectively, up front, to assess whether or not the elements of a project are in place for success.

- Concurrently, to examine why a project may be losing traction.

- Retroactively, to identify lessons learned and improve future project execution.

When we teach the concepts to employees involved with projects, they typically seize on this application quickly. Many even create a new verb to describe the process: *"We need to P-7 this project before we get started."* Such enthusiasm results from P-7's safeguarding against frustrations many have experienced on prior project assignments.

The P-7 Worksheets for Projects are provided on pages 89 and 92. In them you'll see that, as before, the P-7 factors remain consistent as the wording shifts to adapt to multiple applications.

PROSPECTIVE PROJECT REVIEW (SAMPLE)

The first P-7 Project Worksheet you'll see after you turn this page is designed for use on the front-end of a project. As you've seen, you can also use it on any task assignment.

Use of the worksheet is illustrated by the scenario and sample version of the worksheet on the next two pages. While reading the scenario, imagine that you're a member of a project team charged with streamlining your organization's supply chain.

Scenario

As you and your teammates discuss the project before launch, you identify the following issues:

1. The time line is too short to retrieve the vendor data necessary for redesign. This makes the project both unrealistic and under-resourced (available time). P1 would be a "no."

2. Quantitative goals, spelling out cost savings, time savings and synergies are in place; however, qualitative goals (vendor relationship management, quality assurance) have not been clarified. Your team is currently guessing at what senior management might want. P2 would also be a "no."

3. There does not appear to be a single source of quality feedback for the project team. There are multiple stakeholders, with different priorities for the final project configuration, who may be providing inconsistent feedback to the team. P3 is a "no."

4. Some of the data you need to evaluate and modify the current supply chain is tightly controlled by the financial department. The CFO is reluctant to share much information with your team, and the finance representative on your team has little authority to provide necessary data. P4 is likewise a "no."

5. The team is aware of senior management's priority for this project. It is highly visible; so, while recognition is possible for success, failing would not look good for any team members. The team also understands why this project is important to the future competitiveness of the organization and how it affects multiple areas across the corporation. P5 is a "yes."

6. The team is composed of bright, talented people from several constituencies. So far, all team members have shown a willingness to put forth the time and effort to make this a successful initiative. P6 is a "yes."

7. Finally, although the usual corporate politics and silos are present, you are unaware of any other outside influences that could be barriers to the team's project success. P7 is a "yes."

PERFORMANCE-7™ ANALYSIS WORKSHEET

PROSPECTIVE TASK/PROJECT ANALYSIS

Project ___Supply-Chain Reorganization___

Start date ___March 1, 2007___

P-7 Analysis Questions

Answer each question as honestly as possible. Anything other than a completely firm "Yes" must be answered "No."

PERFORMANCE FACTOR	Yes	No
P1 Is execution of this project designed for success? Is this project realistic and well structured? Are adequate resources committed to the project?	—	√
P2 Are expectations clear and matching? • Consistent, clear set of expectations? • Stakeholders in agreement of expectations & priorities?	—	√
P3 Is there a mechanism for timely, quality feedback? • Progress checks in place? • Measurements to provide accurate, unbiased feedback?	—	√
P4 Does the project team possess or have access to skills/knowledge necessary for success? • Knowledge & skills to perform to expectations? • Any skills or information missing?	—	√
P5 Does the project team understand the importance of the task both personally and to the organization? • Realize gains/costs of good/poor performance (WIIFM and WNIIFM)? • Understand importance of task to the organization?	√	—
P6 Is this team capable and willing to perform the task to expectations? • Physically, mentally & emotionally able to perform the task well? • Willing to perform to expectations?	√	—
P7 Can outside issues be ruled out as factors interfering with performance? • Transitory personal problems? • Transitory organizational problems?	√	—

In the real world, the P-7 process is best applied when team members each complete a worksheet, then share/discuss their perceptions until the team reaches consensus. In the example, the team consensus is that this project is on wobbly footing coming out of the starting gate.

The "no" answers on P1, P2, P3, and P4 don't bode well for a smashing success. The team should attempt to change each of these answers to a "yes" before beginning execution.

Immediate Application

Pick a new assignment or an upcoming task you will have to complete. Use the prospective task/project worksheet to analyze how well prepared you are, on the front-end, to complete the assignment/task successfully. If your analysis points to P-7 issues, assume the role of the "squeaky wheel."

CONCURRENT OR RETROSPECTIVE PROJECT REVIEW (SAMPLE)

The second P-7 Project Review Worksheet is designed for use either during an ongoing project or as a "post-mortem" to assess whether or not critical support elements were appropriately in place during project execution. This analysis allows you to make mid-course corrections or capture the learning and avoid support issues on subsequent projects.

Scenario

This application of P-7 to a project will quickly become clear if you assume that the previous example of supply-chain redesign had not gone through a prospective P-7 project review on the front end. The project would be underway, but fighting against some serious constraints.

Envision you and your colleagues six months into the project, as the project is losing traction. This would be an example of Concurrent Analysis use.

An alternative is to see yourself looking back at a project that was less than successful—in which there was a fair amount of both headache and heartache on the part of the project team. Here the mode of usage would be Retrospective Analysis.

You shouldn't have to go further than this to realize why the prospective analysis is so important. Finding out that you are poorly configured for success six months into a project is certainly better than doing nothing. Consider, however, how much time and energy are wasted—and how difficult it is to get back on track and catch up at that point—compared to analysis on the front end.

Also better than doing nothing, but much less effective than Concurrent Analysis, is waiting until project completion to undertake a Retrospective Analysis. Its value is that it captures learning and avoids future missteps. However, it is a tremendous waste of resources and fails to give the organization what it needed: effective execution of a new supply-chain process.

The P-7 Worksheet for Current or Retrospective Project Analysis appears on the next page. Note that it is very similar to the worksheet for prospective analysis. The only difference is that question wording shifts to adapt to the different perspective and time frame.

WILLIAM E BEANE, Ph.D.

PERFORMANCE-7™ ANALYSIS WORKSHEET
CURRENT/RETROSPECTIVE PROJECT ANALYSIS

Project ___*Supply-Chain Reorganization*___

Start date ___*August 1, 2007*___

P-7 Analysis Questions
Answer each question as honestly as possible. Anything other than a completely firm "Yes" must be answered "No."

PERFORMANCE FACTOR	Yes	No
P1 Is/was execution of this project designed for success? Is/was this project realistic and well structured? Are/were adequate resources committed to the project?	_	√
P2 Are/were expectations clear and matching? ▪ Consistent, clear set of expectations? ▪ Stakeholders in agreement of expectations & priorities?	_	√
P3 Is/was there a mechanism for timely, quality feedback? ▪ Progress checks in place? ▪ Measurements to provide accurate, unbiased feedback?	_	√
P4 Does/did the project team possess or have access to skills/ knowledge necessary for success? ▪ Knowledge & skills to perform to expectations? ▪ Any skills or information missing?	_	√
P5 Does/did the project team understand the importance of the task both personally and to the organization? ▪ Realize gains/costs of good/poor performance (WIIFM and WNIIFM)? ▪ Understand importance of task to the organization?	√	_
P6 Is/was this team capable and willing to perform the task to expectations? ▪ Physically, mentally & emotionally able to perform the task well? ▪ Willing to perform to expectations?	√	_
P7 Can/could outside issues be ruled out as factors interfering with performance? ▪ Transitory personal problems? ▪ Transitory organizational problems?	√	_

92

SUMMARY

Employees can be much more proactive in identifying and addressing the factors that they need for success when:

- Being proactive is an expectation of their job.
- It's safe to speak up and ask for support.
- They know P-7 and therefore know how to identify what they have or yet need.

Assuming that managers also know how to use P-7 principles to guide performance, issues should seldom arise.

Empowering employees to seek the elements necessary for their success increases performance, motivation and self-leadership. P-7 becomes an enabling system to build this engagement and empowerment in the workforce.

By extension, project teams can also analyze what they need against what is currently available and take action to secure necessary resources for success. It's best done prospectively, but mid-stream or retrospective analysis is better than nothing, as long as the learning is captured.

IMMEDIATE APPLICATION

You'll find blank versions of both Task/Project Worksheets (prospective and concurrent/retrospective analysis) in the Appendix.

To achieve the full benefits of these tools, use them prior to, during and after every project to ensure that the projects you and your coworkers undertake have optimal success and that the learning is captured.

NEXT . . . THE (MOST) USUAL SUSPECTS

How often is each P-7 factor implicated in performance problems? What factors are missing most often? How often do these factors exist in real life as determinants of successful performance?

You'll find the answers to these questions and more in the next chapter. It presents a brief recap of research we've done over the years on the availability of P-7 factors. The chapter concludes with a discussion of causal analysis and improvement methods.

CHAPTER 13

WHY PERFORMANCE-7™ IS CRITICAL

This chapter discusses why the P-7 analysis and tactics are so important, plus what our real-world data and research say about their use versus lack of use.

IMPORTANCE OF PERFORMANCE LEADERSHIP

It's an obvious fact of life that organizations rise or fall based on their ability to execute effectively. Strategies become pipe dreams and plans turn into confetti when performance is ineffective.

Gaps in performance are much more than an inconvenience or annoyance. Ongoing performance gaps have very real and often significant costs for performers, managers and organizations. That fact is underscored in surveys of managers attending P-7 System workshops.

Managers surveyed estimate that they spend from 30 to 50 percent of their time dealing with performance issues. Here's how that data was collected.

During our performance workshops, one of the first exercises is to have managers do a "quick and dirty" cost analysis of the actual financial cost of their ongoing performance issue. We ask them to look at the direct costs: the costs of wasted time, materials and resources when the job is done inefficiently or has to be redone.

We then focus them on the indirect costs: the radiating impact on current and future business opportunities and customer satisfaction. It's not uncommon for their estimates,which must be verified with their manager, to hit at least four figures. In our experience, a group of 14 to 15 managers, each assessing just one ongoing performance issue, often projects a total annualized impact running up to six or seven figures.

For the majority of managers, this is a powerful eye-opener. Managers have neither been expected, nor trained, to view performance problems as actual business costs. They simply don't think about performance issues in these terms.

While managers are often aware of the "personal costs" of poor performance—frustration, distraction and lowered productivity, they're not aware of the financial impact. They may focus their attention quickly on the cost of missing a customer deadline, but seldom consider the costs of ongoing mediocre performance by a direct report in a particular area.

This is one reason why, as observed earlier, we can look at a performance problem and say: *"Ain't this a shame...I should do something about this"*—then continue ignoring the problem. Although our intentions are invariably to *"Fix this problem later, when I have adequate time to focus on it better,"* too often, we never find adequate time; and the problem lives on and replicates.

LESS OBVIOUS COSTS

There are additional, more insidious costs of ongoing performance problems. When you allow performance problems to continue, you aren't just seen as "too busy" by your direct reports. They perceive you as being unfair or inept. It's very difficult to command trust and respect from staff when they see that you allow performance issues or mediocre performance to continue, without taking action.

In such instances, you're damaging not only trust and respect, you also lose people's commitment, enthusiasm, initiative; and, perhaps eventually, you lose the people themselves. Remember that, typically, it's the most committed and more dedicated members of your team who are carrying the poor performers. They will come to resent your "unfair" failure to address the issue; consequently, their engagement with you and their job decreases. They are also the ones with the most options to leave.

Consider how difficult gaining others' commitment becomes when they perceive that you aren't committed to nurturing high performance and ensuring that each person carries his or her part of the team's load. As Dick Brown, the former CEO of EDS, has notably observed: *"Managers get the performance they tolerate."*

When we tolerate poor performance, we get just that—plus a lot of other negative baggage and headaches. To summarize: Managers are aware of most performance problems but are not always aware of their costs.

WHY P-7 TACTICS ARE CRITICAL

In the absence of a simple but structured system like P-7 to analyze and improve performance, we find repeatedly at all levels of an organization, that:

- Performance issues don't get addressed in a timely fashion.
- Performance analysis is either missing or inaccurate.
- Managers don't understand their role as performance leaders.
- Performance issues don't get addressed in a timely fashion.

Today's Manager

As a manager in today's business environment, you have multiple demands on your time and talents. In between virtual and real meetings, you have to multi-task and constantly re-prioritize on the run in order to fulfill the demands of your job.

Management has never been easy, but it's now getting tougher. A constant flow of emails, voice mails, faxes and instant messages keeps managers on the run. Technology, rather than lightening the load, has raised the background noise level and complexity of the business environment while constricting the time schedule. Everything appears to be a top priority . . . required 24/7 . . . in real time . . . and instantaneously.

Somehow, in the midst of this everything-is-a-priority avalanche, you are supposed to find the time to analyze and improve performance—in addition to getting your "real work" done—even though your team of eight now handles what a department of 13 used to do before the most recent cost-saving restructuring.

You're held accountable for numerous goals and objectives. Then you're measured against these objectives, and those measurements impact other factors such as your compensation and promotability. It's unlikely however, that anyone is going to hold you accountable by asking: *"Did you coach George last week?"* Guess what priority you gradually assign to performance management?

Your "Too-hard" Box

Like many managers, you might have both an in-box and an out-box on your desk. But, you also have another box, hidden from view, way back in the dark corners of the desktop. It's called the "too-hard" box.

Most things that find their way into the too-hard box never emerge. It's where we put those tasks that we find too difficult or too vexing— often the tasks that we haven't done successfully in the past.

Dealing with performance problems often winds up in our too-hard box. Cobwebs are spun and mold grows on such issues before they see the light of day again. When we do decide to tackle a performance issue, we aren't always successful. Even though our intentions may be golden, our tactics and actions range from superficial . . . to misaligned . . . to just plain wrong.

Why Managers Fail

The main reason managers don't succeed in solving performance problems is that they don't know where to start. There are so many factors that could be determining why George or Alice isn't performing that we scarcely know where to start.

Without a system like P-7 to guide our efforts, we cast about, searching for the elusive silver-bullet solution to our performance gap. Unfortunately, we often don't search long enough or far enough because we're convinced we already know what's causing the problem.

BLAMING THE PERFORMER . . . THE ROLE OF ATTRIBUTION

For years, psychologists have studied how people try to explain the behavior that occurs as life unfolds around them. This area of psychology, called "psychology of attribution," deals with how we attribute the causes of behavior, both our own and the behavior of others.

From all of the research on attribution, one principle stands above all others: We attribute the behavior of others differently than we attribute our own . . . even when the behaviors are much the same and occur in similar situations. This difference is so profound and consistent that psychologists call it: the fundamental error of attribution.

97

This fundamental error is this: When explaining the causes of others' behavior, we invoke different explanations than when explaining the exact same behavior on our part. Furthermore—another bolt of the expected obvious—these differing explanations are usually somewhat self-serving.

When explaining why anyone might act in a certain way, we can either attribute the cause to the person:

"Fred was upset with others this morning because he's so moody… particularly in the morning."

Or, we can attribute the behavior to the situation:

"Fred was upset this morning because he was caught in heavy traffic, had car trouble, had a flat time, missed his train, etc."

In short, we either explain behavior as coming from the person, a "personal" attribution; or from the situation, a "situational" attribution. Virtually all of us have a built-in, natural bias that causes us to over-attribute the behavior of others to the person (it's because of them), while attributing the exact same behavior in ourselves to the situation (factors beyond our control).

The factors invoked to explain this bias go beyond our scope here, but they involve things such as different information availability and differing frames of reference. Suffice it to say, this bias is very real and pervasive.

For example: While *you* were late to work because of unavoidable traffic problems, *your colleagues* were late to work because they didn't plan ahead and leave earlier. . . *You* missed the deadline because the project time line was unreasonable, while *she* missed it because she didn't try hard enough . . .*You* slipped because the floor was slick; *he* slipped because he's clumsy.

Getting the picture? We do this constantly, with neither awareness of our bias nor much careful thought and analysis. When we see someone stumble, the label "clumsy" flashes through our consciousness in nanoseconds—far too quickly for any objective analysis to take place. As you will see shortly, it's even wired into our language.

MISATTRIBUTING THE CAUSE OF A PERFORMANCE GAP

Because of the natural, fundamental error of attribution, how likely are we to over-attribute the causes of a performance problem to the performer? We're not only highly likely to do that, it's almost an autonomic reflex, like a knee-jerk reaction. We don't even have to think about it. How often have you overheard dialogue like this?

"What's bothering you Tom? You seem upset."

"Well, I really needed those lab tests this morning, but Gary was late again with them and some were botched. I've just about had it with Gary. I don't know what's wrong with him, but this has to change, or I'm going to his boss."

"I don't blame you . . . no one should have to put up with this."

Such thinking betrays an all-too-common reaction to that kind of a performance problem. But note what just happened. What's Tom's implicit, almost automatic explanation for why Gary was late again?

"I don't know what's wrong with him."

Gary has been indicted, tried and found guilty in the blink of an eye. This quick diagnosis flies in the face of Deming's admonition that many performance problems have little or nothing to do with the performer.

We don't just misattribute the causes of behavior with individuals, we do the same with groups:

"Got a problem John?"

"Yeah, my marketing team is late with the research data we need for the roll-out. I don't know why they can't seem to get their act together, but I've about had it. I don't think they care whether we get this product launched on time or not!"

Notice how naturally . . . how easily . . . how smoothly . . . these statements roll off the tongue. *"It's **their** fault"* is the first explanation of choice for just about any troubling performance gap.

No matter if it's individuals, teams, other departments or entire organizations, we tend to blame first and ask questions later.

How often, for example, would you expect to hear this:

"What's bothering you, Carol? You seem upset."

"Well, I really needed those reports this morning, but Roger was late again with them."

"Carol, no one should have to put up with that."

"I know, but in thinking it through, I realize that I own a big part of this problem."

"How's that?"

"Well . . . I don't know if Roger knew for certain that I needed them this morning."

"I simply told him 'Early this week' assuming that he'd know that meant today. And . . . he probably didn't know I needed the distribution numbers this time along with the shipping data. I forgot to explain to him why I needed the distribution figures, so he probably thought the shipping data would suffice. So, as I said, I probably own a big part of this foul-up."

Don't hold your breath, waiting to observe this lightning bolt of self-realization—unless the other person is incredibly insightful or has been through P-7 training.

Over the years, the most profound impact of P-7 training is often a single self-realization: Managers realize that they, themselves, not their direct reports or colleagues, are responsible for at least part of many performance gaps.

ONE FINAL ATTRIBUTION EFFECT

One final wrinkle in how we attribute the causes of performance gaps is that even more bias occurs when the problem has negative effects for us. Our tendency to over-attribute the actions of others to themselves (the person) is amplified when their actions have undesirable implications for us.

This fact was documented by the late, great Social Psychologist, Fritz Heider, who called it "personalism."

The following scenario exemplifies Heider's personalim:

It's a Saturday morning in the parking lot at your local supermarket. The day is rainy, foggy, drizzly and visibility isn't great. You notice a car begin to back out of its spot and WHAM . . . right into the side of an oncoming car.

It's just a fender-bender, and you can certainly commiserate that the driver backing out couldn't see well—his mirror was fogged over; he didn't mean to do it, etc. When it's not our ox that's gored, it's amazing how objective we can be at times.

Now envision a similar scenario, except, in this one, the driver backed into your brand-new car as you were driving past. You would be outraged:

"How did this idiot get a driver's license! Doesn't he ever look where he's going? He wasn't paying enough attention and certainly doesn't care much about other people's property (and so on…)."

The situation—poor weather and visibility—barely gets noticed!

ATTRIBUTION ERRORS IN THE WORKPLACE

Workplace attribution errors are all too common. To illustrate, suppose someone on your team appears to have dropped the ball. Even worse, the error makes you look bad in front of your boss.

How likely are you to be totally objective, impartial and fair when assessing and attributing the causes of this problem? In this situation, there will probably be few shreds of objectivity left in your performance analysis (pre P-7). We quickly move into becoming the judge, jury (and executioner).

NAÏVE PERFORMANCE ANALYSIS: THE TWO USUAL SUSPECTS

Managers don't always attribute performance gaps to the performer. There's a second diagnosis that's also quite popular: *"He/She needs more training."*

Blaming the performer and calling for training are the two touchstones of what P-7 consultants call "naïve performance analysis."

Note in the following two examples that both are fairly face-saving and protective:

"It's not my fault that Tom doesn't care about his work . . . or that Cynthia didn't get the training she needed from the company."

Before being introduced to P-7, managers repeatedly invoke either *"training problems"* or *"something wrong with the performer"* for most performance issues. If this weren't troublesome enough, they next make these misdiagnoses the basis for planning and executing misguided improvement efforts.

ONE LAST TIME . . . WHO OWNS WHAT?

Before leaving the topic of attribution, there's another key issue to work through if you're somewhat uncomfortable with the earlier analysis in which most of the responsibility for ensuring performance success factors rested with the manager.

Where, you may be asking, is the responsibility of the employee in this equation? Shouldn't the employee, faced with a deficit in one or more of these factors, step forward and ask for what's needed? It's a fair question that deserves a straightforward answer.

While employees may step up to the plate and ask for the P-7 factors in a perfect organizational world, it's not a very prevalent behavior in the business worlds we have encountered. This is particularly true at lower levels of the organization where line employees live and breathe. Such employees have been acculturated and socialized to stay quiet and not rock the boat when support is inadequate, expectations are vague, if feedback comes but once a year (if that) or training is inadequate.

Consider how often an employee is described as "griping," as "a problem child" or labeled as having "a bad attitude" because they have dared to speak up—no matter whether it's about a support deficiency, a poorly designed task, or lack of training or equipment in the workplace.

Speaking up to complain about ineffective processes, ambiguous expectations, scarce feedback, inadequate training or lack of perspective and understanding doesn't usually earn an "employee of the month" merit badge. In fact, researchers who study why employees don't speak up, offer suggestions or ask for help have noted that managers often see such behavior as implicit criticism of their management and react accordingly.

Often, implicit expectations and organizational reward systems maintain an environment in which people are trained to "grin and bear it" instead of speaking up and demanding performance leadership from their managers and organization. When they do bring up problems, they may be laughed at, given a label, or ignored with the same old corporate adage: *"We'll get back to you on that."*

In far too many unenlightened companies, pointing out organizational deficiencies is anything but a sure-fire strategy for career advancement. People assume that if management wanted to fix the problem, it would get fixed, so why keep wasting your breath.

There's no question that the responsibility for ensuring that the P-7 factors are in play does shift as an employee advances in maturity, sophistication and experience level. So, it's to be expected that a senior vice president of marketing would ask a CEO for clarification if goals were unclear. Likewise, a senior researcher could be expected to demand appropriate training if none had been made available.

Such situations don't detract from the fact, however, that, for the vast majority of employees, the manager is responsible for providing the P-7 factors that support performance. Employees shouldn't have to beg and plead. At the end of the day the "performance buck" always stops at the manager's desk.

RESEARCH FINDINGS ON PERFORMANCE-7 FACTORS

Unfortunately, when we look back over a summary of data from almost a decade of performance workshops, begging and pleading tend to look like reasonable options. While conducting those workshops, we've been gathering 360-degree feedback data from managers and their direct reports.

Survey data allows us to compare the perceptions of managers and their direct reports regarding the presence or absence of P-7 factors in the workplace. In surveys, we've asked managers how often—what percentage of time—they felt that each factor was provided; we asked employees how often, also in percentage of time, they felt that each factor was effectively present.

WILLIAM E BEANE, Ph.D.

The table below summarizes survey responses from workshops over a 10-year time span. It represents input from more than 600 managers and over 3000 employees.

SURVEY DATA
FREQUENCY OF USE – P-7 PERFORMANCE SUCCESS FACTORS

	PERCENTAGE OF TIME	
P-7 FACTOR	Managers	Employees
P1: Task designed for success	78	64
P2: Clear, matching performance expectations	84	38
P3: Timely, balanced feedback	65	43
P4: Adequate skills and knowledge (competency)	77	68
P5: Understanding task importance – personal	94	71
P5: Understanding task importance – organizational	73	57

This summary of data should not be regarded as being highly scientific or precise because the questions eliciting responses varied over the years. The pattern, however, is highly congruent with the content of P-7 System performance case discussions with managers and line employees over the past several years.

104

Data Interpretation

Some significant points that the data reflects are:

1. Managers' and employees' perceptions of the presence of P-7 factors differ dramatically. As might be expected, managers are far more optimistic about their presence.

2. Task design is in better shape than most other factors, but employees still feel that more than one-third of the time, they are dealing with inadequate task design on the job.

3. The weakest practices are expectations and feedback, respectively. As mentioned earlier, consider the combined impact of both of these factors being missing for roughly 6 out of 10 employees. Their impact on performance is staggering. Recall earlier the problems caused when expectations are not aligned. The only thing that aligns them is feedback.

4. Competence is one of the stronger factors, but even the optimistic estimate of managers indicates that almost one-fourth of the time, employees haven't received the skills and knowledge necessary for satisfactory task performance. Employees feel that this is missing almost one-third of the time—hardly an inspiring state of affairs.

5. Although understanding of personal gains/costs is fairly high, relative to the other factors, understanding of organizational importance is quite low. Almost half of the employees in the sample didn't understand the importance of their jobs to organizational strategy and outcomes for customers. Consider the impact this has on deadlines, quality, service and employee engagement over time. These are incredibly high costs for such an easily addressed problem.

Why P-7 Factors Aren't Employed More Often

Most managers view the P-7 factors as being common sense; but, as the data indicates, using the factors is far from common practice. The logical question therefore arises: Why do reasonable managers who agree that the P-7 factors are important—and that they support higher performance—fail to employ the P-7 factors more religiously?

At least part of the answer to this question can be found in Pfeffer and Sutton's book "The Knowing-Doing Gap." The authors outline several of the problems that separate knowing from doing. Two of the issues they identify have a strong impact on the absence of performance leadership:

- Talk replaces action.
- Having procedures builds reassurance.

Along the cubicles and hallways of any business, you hear much discussion of issues related to performance. Topics ranging from the importance of hitting this quarter's numbers to the need for quick turnaround for Friday's deadline include discussion and debate centering on performance. Ask managers what's keeping them awake at night, and you're likely to hear some variation of a story about how a team of three is now struggling to handle the former workload of six.

Discussions of performance and performance-related issues may fill the air; yet, as the preceding table illustrates, employees still work with unclear priorities, wait for feedback that doesn't arrive and remain clueless as to why one initiative is more important than another.

Every medium to large company—and most small companies—have some type of performance management procedures in place. Most are centered on annual goals and have a yearly performance appraisal that reviews progress. Nicely designed forms are completed, signed and put in the drawer; but, on a day-to-day basis, real performance leadership falls short.

Senior management is reassured that "performance is being managed" by the summaries and reports from HR outlining how many appraisals have been completed. Down in the trenches, however, we all know what's really happening—or not happening. The question is

"How is it, or why isn't it, happening?"

CHAPTER 14

P-7 ANALYSIS: PERFORMANCE MANAGEMENT PERFORMANCE GAP

Performance Management: How is it, or why isn't it, happening?

Our data and discussion have identified a gap in performance leadership between what is needed and what is actually happening. We therefore have a perfect candidate for a model P-7 analysis.

You might want to answer the questions we're about to pose for your own organization as we progress though the P-7 process. By now, you should be thoroughly familiar with it.

IDENTIFYING THE GAP

As we've done earlier, we'll summarize our answers using the Organizational Issue Worksheet—beginning by identifying the gap.

Expected Gap

Performance leadership should be occurring on a regular basis throughout the organization to maximize organizational effectiveness and efficiency.

Actual Gap

In most organizations, performance leadership is not practiced as a priority, taking second or third place behind other "more essential" leadership activities.

P1 QUESTION:
IS THE TASK OF PERFORMANCE LEADERSHIP DESIGNED FOR SUCCESS?

The major factor here is whether or not managers have adequate time to lead performance. In today's lean organizations, many first-line and middle managers have precious little time to manage anyone. They may have a manager's title, but they often function primarily as individual contributors, doing the same work as their direct reports.

For many such managers, time is a realistic barrier. The answer to the P1 question has to be "no."

P2 QUESTION:
ARE EXPECTATIONS FOR PERFORMANCE LEADERSHIP CLEAR & MATCHING?

Although performance leadership receives ample lip service and the annual appraisal session might be documented, the daily and weekly activities of performance leadership are not set as priorities in most organizations.

In their outstanding book, "EXECUTION: The Discipline of Getting Things Done," Larry Bossidy and Ram Charon point out that coaching and developing people are top priorities of a leader. Jack Welch, retired CEO of General Electric, repeatedly demonstrated that developing people was his top priority as he led GE to exceptional success.

If every manager in your company were asked to list their top five priorities, how many would include performance leadership? Although our data is based on a smaller sample, other researchers have validated the problem that exists with clear expectations.

In a study released during March, 2005, Microsoft looked at responses from 38,000 participants in 200 countries during its Personal Productivity Challenge initiative. Among other factors, the results indicated that: "... *among the most common productivity pitfalls are unclear objectives.*"

It's one of the great ironies of business that, while producing successful results is always a priority, undertaking the straightforward performance leadership practices necessary to get those results is seldom a priority. Most organizations succeed . . . *not because* of their efforts in performance leadership but *in spite of* them. Companies that make it clear they expect it and make it a high priority almost always lead their competitors.

Companies significantly trailing their industrial leaders invariably have no clear and matching expectations for performance leadership. The answer to the P2 Question is therefore "no."

P3 QUESTION: IS FEEDBACK PRESENT?

If, as noted earlier, expectations for performance leadership are usually missing, you can certainly be safe in betting that feedback will be at least equally absent. In our performance workshops, we often pose managers with a question they've never heard before: *"Other than a call from HR saying they're missing someone's annual appraisal form, how many of you get feedback on how well you manage performance?"*

Nary a hand is raised. We usually get a similar response to a follow-on question: *"How many of you ever get feedback from either your reports or your boss on how well you manage performance—other than when one of your people has made a mistake?"*

Since senior management doesn't make performance leadership an explicit expectation, why would anyone be giving feedback on how well you're doing? Employees who have been largely acculturated to be quiet and compliant certainly aren't going to bring up any problems with how you manage them. They know better than that, because they know that in the jungle of corporate survival, when it comes to performance issues: *"No news is good news."*

It's bad news, however, in the answer to the P3 question. The headline reads: Still another "no."

P4 QUESTION:
ARE SKILLS AND KNOWLEDGE (COMPETENCY) PRESENT?

The answer to Question P4 is less clear than the answers to the first three questions and appears to vary considerably from one company to the next. Although most companies provide some kind of supervisory or interpersonal skill training, many give little or no time to performance management training. Recall that most training in "performance appraisal" is focused on how to correctly complete and document the paperwork and/or how to conduct the annual appraisal.

So, managers are often trained in how to use the computerized appraisal system, then presented with some guidelines for appraisal discussions; but that's about it. Given the inherent difficulty of dealing with performance problems and managers' lack of skills in this area, it should come as no surprise when issues don't get addressed.

Fred Smith, CEO of Federal Express, summed up the state of affairs years ago when he remarked:

"We're using the words 'hard' and 'soft' wrong. The hard stuff's easy . . . it's the soft stuff that's hard."

Given the choice between wading into a difficult performance issue and doing next quarter's budget forecast, most managers will say: "Let's have another look at that spreadsheet."

The bottom line is that most organizations are remiss in performance leadership training. As a result, it's a "no" response again to the P4 question.

P5 QUESTION:
IS THERE UNDERSTANDING OF PERSONAL AND ORGANIZATIONAL TASK IMPORTANCE

This question requires a two-part answer in order to address both issues separately. Let's start with personal importance.

Personal Importance

Do managers really see a personal gain for themselves in practicing performance leadership activities? As before, a few probably do; but most don't.

Much of this posture is based on the perceived poor cost-benefit ratio of performance leadership activities. They take time, may not have quick results, can be adversarial and difficult and often don't appear to have a lasting beneficial impact on performance.

Our informal observations confirm that many managers have "thrown in the towel" on coaching activities because they don't feel that the time and "pain" are worth the gain. While the personal payoff and benefits of performance leadership are perceived as weak, there are few, if any, consequences for not engaging in such behaviors.

Managers usually take action if there's a performance problem or during a crisis. However, since they receive no reprimands for failing to provide performance leadership on a day-to-day basis, few take the time to do it.

In the real world of organizations, how often would a manager be asked questions like:

"Did you coach George this week?" . . . *"Have you clarified expectations for Joan?"*

Unless a critical project time line is being abused or customer deadlines are being missed, you know the answer. Most managers devote the majority of their time and attention to the tasks that they are measured against.

In short, many middle managers don't hold their direct reports accountable for performance leadership and don't supply it themselves. And it's pretty clear why. They don't see any personal gains for doing it, compared to the costs—and expect few consequences for not doing it.

Organizational Importance

When painting the picture of organizational importance, it doesn't get much prettier than on the personal side. As discussed earlier, when examining lack of expectations, organizations may give lip service to the importance of performance leadership, but they don't really mean it.

Conclusion

Since the P-7 factors are interactive, by now, it's probably becoming obvious that if there are no expectations for an activity, if no feedback is given, and if there's not much emphasis on training for competency, employees will invariable conclude that this activity can't be too important to the organization.

Since that's the case with most organizations, our hand is forced in answering the P5 question. It has to be "no."

P6 AND P7 QUESTIONS

P6 is probably not an issue. Most managers are capable of leading performance and willing to do it when they have the right skills.

P7 is not applicable to an organizational-level analysis.

GAP ANALYSIS SUMMARY

A summary of the preceding gap analysis is provided in the Organizational Worksheet on the next page.

PERFORMANCE-7™ ANALYSIS WORKSHEET

ORGANIZATIONAL ISSUE

GAP – Expected	GAP – Actual
Performance leadership should be provided regularly across the organization for maximum productivity.	*Performance leadership is not practiced as a priority, taking 2nd/3rd place behind "more essential" activities.*

P-7 Analysis Questions

Answer each question as honestly as possible. Anything other than a completely firm "Yes" must be answered "No."

PERFORMANCE FACTOR	Yes	No
P1 Is this organozational task designed for success? Is it realistic and well structured? Are adequate resources committed to it?	—	√
P2 Are expectations clear and matching across the organization? ▪ Staff fully understands expectations? ▪ Expectations/priorities match?	—	√
P3 Has timely, quality feedback been given across the organization? ▪ *Positive* feedback to motivate & reinforce expectations? ▪ *Constructive* feedback to get back on track; clarify expectations?	—	√
P4 Are individuals competent to perform the task? ▪ Possess the *skills?* ▪ Possess the *knowledge & experience?*	—	√
P5 Does staff fully understand the importance of the task both personally and to the organization? ▪ Realize gains/costs of good/poor performance (WIIFM and WNIIFM)? ▪ Understand importance of task to the organization?	—	√
P6 Is staff capable and willing to perform the task to expectations? ▪ Physically, mentally & emotionally able to perform the task well? ▪ Willing to perform to expectations?	— NA —	
P7 Can outside issues be ruled out as factors interfering with performance? ▪ Transitory personal problems? ▪ Transitory organizational problems?	— NA —	

A SAD SUMMARY

It's not surprising that performance leadership isn't consistently practiced across most organizations. Our P-7 analysis points out significant problems with every one of the first five factors, leaving little confusion as to why performance leadership doesn't occur at an acceptable level.

Even if managers were capable and willing—and unhindered by personal agendas—it still should come as no surprise that performance leadership is so often inadequate. As noted earlier, organizations achieve results in spite of their performance leadership practices, not because of them.

A MORE HOPEFUL VISION

You work in an imperfect world populated with the foibles of humanity and the dysfunctions of organizations. No single analysis and improvement system is going to turn it all into a picture of perfection.

This book, however, can make the picture considerably brighter. You can put the P-7 System and the associated worksheets to use immediately to start building your own P-7 performance culture. You will be amazed at the results.

Best wishes for your future success!

APPENDIX

P-7™ SYSTEM

ALL APPLICATIONS

Guidelines and Worksheets

PERFORMANCE-7 INTERPRETATION GUIDELINES

1. All questions must be answered as objectively as possible and must pertain specifically to the performer. No answer should be assumed, and there should be no easy "yes" answers.

2. "Yes" cannot be the answer to every question. If that were the case, there would be no performance gap! Everything necessary for performance would be present, and you would not be trying to solve a performance problem.

3. If the answers to P1 through P5 are "yes" and there is still a performance gap, you need to make a change:

   - If capability is the issue, a change in the performer's position

   - If willingness is the issue, initiating steps terminating the performer's employment

   - If personal issues are interfering with performance, getting the employee involved with HR.

   Those are the only three options left.

4. If any of the answers for P1 through P5 are "no, " go back and reexamine them before going any further. It is difficult—if not impossible—to answer P6 because anything missing from the P1–P5 factors looks exactly like a problem in capability or willingness in how they impact performance.

P-7 SYSTEM WORKSHEETS

The following pages contains worksheets for use in dealing with:

- Direct reports.
- Peers or colleagues.
- Team issues.
- Organizational issues.
- Prospective task/project analysis.
- Current/retrospective project analysis.

The worksheets are printed so that they can be used as stand-alone forms, with the working section on the front and an area for note-taking on the back.

Please feel free to remove these forms from their binding and use them for your personal gap analyses and performance improvement planning. Please also understand that these forms are protected by US copyright law. It is permissible to reproduce the forms for your personal use, but they cannot be mass-produced, sold, or represented to be the intellectual property of any organization other than DB Consulting.

PERFORMANCE-7™ ANALYSIS WORKSHEET
DIRECT REPORT

GAP – Expected

GAP – Actual

P-7 Analysis Questions

*Answer each question as honestly as possible. Anything
other than a completely firm "Yes" must be answered "No."*

PERFORMANCE FACTOR	Yes	No
P1 Is the task designed for success? • Others performing this task well? • Task *realistic*, well *designed*? • Adequate *resources* committed?	—	—
P2 Are expectations clear and matching? • Expectations & standards certain to be fully understood? • Expectations/priorities match?	—	—
P3 Has quality feedback been given: timely, constructive, balanced and honest? • Feedback *positive* to motivate & reinforce expectations? • Feedback *constructive* (gets back on track; clarifies expectations)?	—	—
P4 Does the performer have the competence to perform the task to expectations? • Performer has the *skills?* • Performer has the *knowledge* & *experience*?	—	—
P5 Does the performer understand the importance of the task personally and to the organization? • Performer realizes gains/costs of good/poor performance (WIIFM and WNIIFM)? • Performer knows importance of task to organization/customers?	—	—
P6 Is the performer capable and willing to perform the task to expectations? • Performer capable physically, mentally & emotionally of performing task well? • Performer willing to perform to expectations?	—	—
P7 Can personal issues be ruled out as factors interfering with performance? • Performer experiencing any physical/mental health problems? • Performer having family/financial/substance abuse problems?	—	—

NOTES

_____

_____

_____

_____

_____

_____

_____

PERFORMANCE-7™ ANALYSIS WORKSHEET

PEER/COLLEAGUE

GAP – Expected

GAP – Actual

P-7 Analysis Questions

Answer each question as honestly as possible. Anything other than a completely firm "Yes" must be answered "No."

PERFORMANCE FACTOR	Yes	No
P1 Is this collaboration task designed for success? Is collaboration structured well so it's easier for the peer to give me what I need?	—	—
P2 Are expectations clear and matching? ▪ Peer fully understand my expectations? ▪ Expectations/priorities match?	—	—
P3 Have I given timely, quality feedback? ▪ *Positive* feedback to motivate & reinforce expectations? ▪ *Constructive* feedback to put back on track; clarify expectations?	—	—
P4 Is the peer competent to supply what I need? ▪ Has the *skills?* ▪ Has the *knowledge* & *experience?*	—	—
P5 Does the colleague understand the importance of the task personally and to the organization? ▪ Realizes gains/costs of good/poor performance (WIIFM and WNIIFM)? ▪ Knows importance of task to me and the organization?	—	—
P6 Is the peer capable and willing to perform the task to expectations? ▪ Physically, mentally & emotionally able to perform the task well? ▪ Willing to give me what I need?	—	—
P7 Can personal issues be ruled out as factors interfering with performance? ▪ Transitory problems? ▪ Transitory organizational problems?	—	—

NOTES

_____

_____

_____

_____

_____

_____

_____

PERFORMANCE-7™ ANALYSIS WORKSHEET

TEAM ISSUE

GAP – Expected

GAP – Actual

P-7 Analysis Questions

Answer each question as honestly as possible. Anything other than a completely firm "Yes" must be answered "No."

PERFORMANCE FACTOR	Yes	No
P1 Is this team task designed for success? Is it realistic and well structured? Are adequate resources committed to it?	—	—
P2 Are expectations clear and matching? ▪ Team fully understands my expectations? ▪ Expectations/priorities match?	—	—
P3 Has timely, quality feedback been given to the entire team? ▪ *Positive* feedback to motivate & reinforce expectations? ▪ *Constructive* feedback to get back on track; clarify expectations?	—	—
P4 Is the team competent to perform the task? ▪ Has the *skills*? ▪ Has the *knowledge* & *experience*?	—	—
P5 Do team members fully understand the importance of the task both personally and to the organization? ▪ Realize gains/costs of good/poor performance (WIIFM and WNIIFM)? ▪ Knows importance of task to the organization?	—	—
P6 Is the team capable and willing to perform the task to expectations? ▪ Physically, mentally & emotionally able to perform the task well? ▪ Willing to perform to expectations?	—	—
P7 Can personal issues be ruled out as factors interfering with performance? ▪ Transitory problems? ▪ Transitory organizational problems?	—	—

NOTES

_____

_____

_____

_____

_____

_____

_____

PERFORMANCE-7™ ANALYSIS WORKSHEET

ORGANIZATIONAL ISSUE

GAP – Expected

GAP – Actual

P-7 Analysis Questions

Answer each question as honestly as possible. Anything other than a completely firm "Yes" must be answered "No."

PERFORMANCE FACTOR	Yes	No
P1 Is this organozational task designed for success? Is it realistic and well structured? Are adequate resources committed to it?	—	—
P2 Are expectations clear and matching across the organization? ▪ Staff fully understands expectations? ▪ Expectations/priorities match?	—	—
P3 Has timely, quality feedback been given across the organization? ▪ *Positive* feedback to motivate & reinforce expectations? ▪ *Constructive* feedback to put back on track; clarify expectations?	—	—
P4 Are individuals competent to perform the task? ▪ Possess the *skills?* ▪ Possess the *knowledge & experience?*	—	—
P5 Does staff fully understand the importance of the task both personally and to the organization? ▪ Realize gains/costs of good/poor performance (WIIFM and WNIIFM)? ▪ Understand importance of task to the organization?	—	—
P6 Is staff capable and willing to perform the task to expectations? ▪ Physically, mentally & emotionally able to perform the task well? ▪ Willing to perform to expectations?	—	—
P7 Can outside issues be ruled out as factors interfering with performance? ▪ Transitory personal problems? ▪ Transitory organizational problems?	—	—

NOTES

_____

_____

_____

_____

_____

_____

_____

PERFORMANCE-7™ ANALYSIS WORKSHEET
PROSPECTIVE TASK/PROJECT ANALYSIS

Project _____

Start date _____

P-7 Analysis Questions
Answer each question as honestly as possible. Anything other than a completely firm "Yes" must be answered "No."

PERFORMANCE FACTOR	Yes	No
P1 Is execution of this project designed for success? Is this project realistic and well structured? Are adequate resources committed to the project?	—	—
P2 Are expectations clear and matching? ▪ Consistent, clear set of expectations? ▪ Stakeholders in agreement of expectations & priorities?	—	—
P3 Is there a mechanism for timely, quality feedback? ▪ Progress checks in place? ▪ Measurements to provide accurate, unbiased feedback?	—	—
P4 Does the project team possess or have access to skills/knowledge necessary for success? ▪ Knowledge & skills to perform to expectations? ▪ Any skills or information missing?	—	—
P5 Does the project team understand the importance of the task both personally and to the organization? ▪ Realize gains/costs of good/poor performance (WIIFM and WNIIFM)? ▪ Understand importance of task to the organization?	—	—
P6 Is this team capable and willing to perform the task to expectations? ▪ Physically, mentally & emotionally able to perform the task well? ▪ Willing to perform to expectations?	—	—
P7 Can outside issues be ruled out as factors interfering with performance? ▪ Transitory personal problems? ▪ Transitory organizational problems?	—	—

NOTES

_____

_____

_____

_____

_____

_____

_____

PERFORMANCE-7™ ANALYSIS WORKSHEET

CURRENT/RETROSPECTIVE PROJECT ANALYSIS

Project _____

Start date _____

P-7 Analysis Questions

*Answer each question as honestly as possible. Anything
other than a completely firm "Yes" must be answered "No."*

PERFORMANCE FACTOR	Yes	No
P1 Is/was execution of this project designed for success? Is/was this project realistic and well structured? Are/were adequate resources committed to the project?	—	—

P2 Are/were expectations clear and matching?
  ▪ Consistent, clear set of expectations?
  ▪ Stakeholders in agreement of expectations & priorities?
	—	—

P3 Is/was there a mechanism for timely, quality feedback?
  ▪ Progress checks in place?
  ▪ Measurements to provide accurate, unbiased feedback?
	—	—

P4 Does/did the project team possess or have access to skills/knowledge necessary for success?
  ▪ Knowledge & skills to perform to expectations?
  ▪ Any skills or information missing?
	—	—

P5 Does/did the project team understand the importance of the task both personally and to the organization?
  ▪ Realize gains/costs of good/poor performance (WIIFM and WNIIFM)?
  ▪ Understand importance of task to the organization?
	—	—

P6 Is/was this team capable and willing to perform the task to expectations?
  ▪ Physically, mentally & emotionally able to perform the task well?
  ▪ Willing to perform to expectations?
	—	—

P7 Can/could outside issues be ruled out as factors interfering with performance?
  ▪ Transitory personal problems?
  ▪ Transitory organizational problems?
	—	—

NOTES

_____

_____

_____

_____

_____

_____

_____

Made in the USA
Lexington, KY
01 September 2015